LUCY SUMMERS runs her own successful landscape design partnership, the Open Garden Company, which has both national and international clients. As an RHS-qualified horticulturalist she has staged show gardens at the Chelsea Flower Show and has been awarded much-coveted Gold and Silver medals for her garden designs. She also contributes regularly to gardening publications, gives lectures to gardening clubs and organisations, and co-hosted *Britain's Best Back Gardens* for ITV among other television work. She lives in Surrey.

lease
You c

CHARTER
MARK

CUSTOMER S

" Trying to find a gardening book that is relevant to your needs isn't as straight-forward as it seems. Whether you are new to gardening or a dab hand, sometimes plant descriptions, including care, maintenance and general gardening jargon, can seem overly complicated or, worse still, just too vague. Greenfingers Guides cut through all this, delivering honest, practical information on a wide variety of fruit and veg with easy-to-follow layouts, all designed to enable you to get the best from your garden. Happy gardening! **"**

GREENFINGERS GUIDES
FRUIT AND VEGETABLES

LUCY SUMMERS

headline

Photographs © Garden World Images Ltd
except those listed opposite

The right of Lucy Summers to be identified as the Author
of the Work has been asserted by her in accordance with
the Copyright, Designs and Patents Act 1988.

First published in 2009
by HEADLINE PUBLISHING GROUP

I

Lucy Summers would be happy to hear from readers
with their comments on the book at the following
e-mail address: lucy@greenfingersguides.co.uk

The Greenfingers Guides series concept was originated
by Lucy Summers and Darley Anderson

A CIP catalogue record for this title is available from
the British Library

ISBN 978 0 7553 1761 5

Design by Isobel Gillan
Printed and bound in Italy by Canale & C.S.p.A.

Headline's policy is to use papers that are natural,
renewable and recyclable products and made from wood
grown in sustainable forests. The logging and
manufacturing processes are expected to conform to the
environmental regulations of the country of origin.

HEADLINE PUBLISHING GROUP
An Hachette Livre UK Company
338 Euston Road
London NW1 3BH

www.headline.co.uk
www.hachettelivre.co.uk
www.greenfingersguides.co.uk
www.theopengardencompany.co.uk

PICTURE CREDITS
All photographs supplied by Garden World Images

'Boskoop Glory' (p. 17), Cardoon stalks (p. 48)
© Floramedia; 'Orlando' (p. 38), 'Azur Star' (p. 64) © HILD
samen; 'Fantasia' (p. 11), 'Purpurea' (p. 19), 'Gariguette'
(p. 31) © MAP/Arnaud Descat; 'Versailles Blanche' (p. 29)
© MAP/Nathalie Pasquel; 'Pixie' (p. 46), 'Resistafly' (p. 49),
'Daybreak' (p. 53) © Organic Gardening Catalogue;
'Chelsea' (p. 22), 'Broadview' (p. 32), 'Angers' (p. 85)
© S.E. Marshall & Co Ltd; 'Applause' (p. 88) © Suttons

ACKNOWLEDGEMENTS
My thanks to Darling, Zoe, Serena, Lorraine, Emma, Josh,
Isobel and Charlotte. And to all my wonderful nearest
and dearest.

OTHER TITLES IN THE GREENFINGERS GUIDES SERIES:

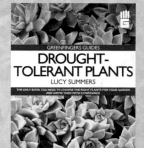

Climbers and Wall Shrubs
ISBN 978 0 7553 1758 5

Drought-Tolerant Plants
ISBN 978 0 7553 1759 2

Contents

Introduction

We all search for happiness: welcome to journey's end! I can guarantee that growing your own fruit and vegetables delivers happiness and contentment by the spadeful. Perhaps it's the chance to get back to the land and immerse ourselves in nature and a simple, honest environment that so appeals to us.

Growing your own fruit and vegetables will save money, and gives you the opportunity to try some of the old-fashioned or unusual varieties that are not widely available in the shops. More of us are choosing to grow our own crops because of concerns about the chemical dangers: you know the provenance of your food is absolutely tip-top when you have nurtured it all the way from seed to harvest. And then there is the sheer pleasure and practicality of the task. Whatever your motives, you are going to love seeing your fruit and vegetable crops grow.

The vast majority of fruit and vegetables are hardy in our climate and the sole contribution you have to make is time, a little patience and vigilance. But before we go any further we do need to do a small reality check. Some years ago, I was showing off my high-maintenance acreage of formal garden to a very wise, wily old gardener, who said to me, as I proudly pointed to my nettle-infested potential veggie plot, 'You don't need a vegetable plot, girl, you need a supermarket.' Point taken. We all have eyes too big for our stomachs and it is easy to imagine you can grow more than you can handle.

It is important to be realistic: a small plot (2m/6ft × 4m/13ft) will need at least two to four hours of attention weekly, whilst a larger area of 125sq m/1,345sq ft (about half of a traditional allotment plot) will take ten hours or more. Be sensible: start out with a limited repertoire of crops in a small space. Choose quick-growing crops that will build up your confidence and give you a speedy return, such as early carrots, lettuces or any of the more exotic salad leaves; peas are ready for harvesting just twelve weeks after sowing. Then increase the range of vegetables as you gain growing experience. Start off modestly and give yourself time to get your hand in. Before you know it you will have taken up your lawn or signed up for an allotment!

Decorative vegetable bed in summer

Allotment culture is a thing apart: I can't recommend it highly enough. People of all ages garden on them, from young couples to retired folk and, by and large, they are productive, sociable and peaceable places. There are nice little perks in growing on an allotment: seeds can be bought or traded, glut crops swapped and compost heaps shared, and you will have the bonus of tapping into some very sound horticultural tutelage from experienced, practical and often humorous fellow growers. Experienced allotment growers are incredibly amenable to advising the novice grower: I have learnt more about the do's and don'ts of veggie growing from the old boys up on the allotment than I could have absorbed from any book.

Every allotment has a 'waste not, want not' crew, who seem to recycle just about every material imaginable. Potting sheds are cobbled together out of an odd assortment of planks, plastic sacking, chicken wire and lord knows what else, and you may see old CDs or polythene bags hung up and flapping about as bird scarers. More gruesomely, I have seen dead birds strung out to deter our feathered friends. There is a lot of folklore in these methods and I am not sure how effective they have proved to be!

In the following pages you will find a wide variety of fruit and vegetables that have been chosen for ease of production and unique flavour, together with one or two more unusual varieties that are also ornamental plants in their own right. Manage your outdoor space, time and crops well and you will enjoy all the benefits of nature's own bountiful harvest.

Using this book

The fruit and vegetables have been ordered alphabetically in two separate sections with descriptions and practical cultivation advice. More detailed information, covering the elements in the profiles, and including help with growing, pruning and pests and diseases, will be found after the plant profiles. Where seasons are mentioned the corresponding months will vary according to local weather patterns, regional differences and the effects of climate change. The table below is based in the British Isles, and is a flexible guide.

Early spring	March	Early autumn	September
Mid-spring	April	Mid-autumn	October
Late spring	May	Late autumn	November
Early summer	June	Early winter	December
Mid-summer	July	Mid-winter	January
Late summer	August	Late winter	February

The tables in the vegetable section indicate sowing, planting and harvesting times. For sowing:
○ indoors ◉ outdoors ◑ indoors *and* outdoors

Skill level is indicated by one of three ratings:
EASY, **MEDIUM** or **TRICKY**

Many of the plants chosen for this book have been given the Award of Garden Merit (AGM) by the Royal Horticultural Society (RHS). This is a really useful pointer in helping you decide which plants to buy. The AGM is intended to be of practical value to the ordinary gardener, and plants that merit the award are the cream of the crop. The RHS are continually assessing new plant cultivars and you can be sure that any plant with an AGM will have excellent decorative features and be:
- easily available to the buying public
- easy to grow and care for
- not particularly susceptible to pests or disease
- robust and healthy

FRUIT

Apple
Malus domestica

EASY

'Ashmead's Kernel'

'Bramley's Seedling'

Apples are the most commonly grown of all fruit trees. They are deciduous trees with attractive spring blossoms and a delicious crop of red, green or russet-coloured crunchy apples for eating or cooking, ripening from July onwards (depending on the variety grown). Apples suit many soils but it is important to choose one that is the right size for the plot and has a good flavour. Running a taste trial with native varieties from the supermarket can help in making a decision and apple growers often have apple-tasting days. They can be grown as isolated trees or trained as fans or espaliers. Most apples are self-sterile, which means they need pollen from another apple tree in flower at the same time in order to produce fruit. A good nursery will ensure you are buying the right tree and advise on suitable pollinators.

VARIETIES 'Ashmead's Kernel' ☻ Lumpy-shaped, rosy-green, old English variety, with excellent, sharp-tasting flavour, ripening from October (needs a pollinator); **'Bramley's Seedling'** ☻ The most widely grown cooking variety with large, irregular, sharp-tasting apples of green flushed red, ripening September to October (needs a pollinator); **'Egremont Russet'** ☻ Crisp, sweet, nutty flavoured dessert apple with sandpaper-textured skin, ripening October (part self-fertile); **'George Neal'** ☻ Kentish variety good for eating and cooking, ripening August to September (needs a pollinator)

ASPECT Sunny, sheltered site, with protection from frosts and winds

SOIL Fertile, deep, moist, well-drained soil; add well-rotted farmyard manure before planting; pH6.0–7.0

PLANTING Plant container-grown plants all year round as long as ground is not frozen or waterlogged (to the same depth as in the pot) and bare-root trees in November to March; bare-root specimens tend to establish more quickly. Install stakes or wires, depending on the form you are growing

CARE Water well until established and mulch the base of the tree in late winter or early spring to conserve moisture in the soil. Keep the base of the tree grass free as this impairs vigour

PRUNING For formative pruning as a free-standing tree, see page 114. Once established, prune in winter, removing dead, diseased or damaged wood and keeping an open centre; this simple maintenance pruning will keep trees bearing generous harvests well into old age

PROBLEMS Capsid bug, caterpillars, codling moth and red spider mite; apple powdery mildew, bitter pit, blossom wilt, canker, scab, *Verticillium* wilt and woolly aphid; wasps

HARVESTING Pick when apples come away from the tree easily

YIELD 18kg/40lb per tree

GREENFINGER TIP *A crab apple planted nearby will act as pollinator for most varieties*

FRUIT

Apricot
Prunus armeniaca

'Alfred'

'Moorpark'

Apricots are a lovely fruit but, truthfully, the site has to be near perfect to get a worthwhile crop. It is a deciduous, spreading, hardy, early-flowering medium-sized (3m/10ft) tree with heart-shaped, mid-green leaves and white blossom, flushed pink, in early to mid-spring and sometimes in late winter, so harvesting times can be unpredictable. It bears delicious, felty-skinnned, sweet, pale orange to yellow, juicy stoned fruits, usually from July to September, but needs to establish for two to four years before fruiting. Apricots are largely self-fertile, but they flower at a time of year when there are few pollinating insects about, so hand pollinating with a brush is sometimes necessary. They can be grown as standard trees, but are just as successful grown as a fan in smaller spaces.

VARIETIES 'Alfred' Medium-sized fruits with sweet orange flesh, ripening early August; '**Moorpark**' ⚥ Sweet, orange fruit with pink blush in August to September

ASPECT Full sun, in a sheltered position, with protection from cold winds

SOIL Fertile, deep, moist, well-drained soil; add organic matter to light soils; pH6.5–7.5

PLANTING Plant container-grown trees all year round as long as ground is not frozen or waterlogged, or plant bare-root trees in October to November. Allow growing space of 4.5–6m/15–20ft for a mature tree and 2.5–4m/8–13ft for a wall-trained specimen. Stake young trees or install wires

CARE In late winter, apply bonemeal or sulphate of potash to the root area. Mulch with organic matter or grass clippings to keep the base weed free and conserve moisture in spring, and remove suckers from the base as you spot them. They need plenty of sunshine and warmth to make a good fruit crop; protect blossom (appearing from March) from frost, otherwise buds may not open, or will fall prematurely. Move container-grown trees around to follow the sun, though large pots are needed as they like a free root run

PRUNING For formative pruning, see page 114. Prune established trees in June and July, removing any crossed, dead or damaged branches and any stems that are congesting the middle of the tree. After harvesting is over, remove any branches that fruited poorly, to stimulate new growth. Paint pruning wounds with a tree sealant

PROBLEMS Brown scale; blossom wilt, dieback and silver leaf; birds

HARVESTING Pick ripe fruit from July to August, when they are slightly soft (though this stage varies depending on the warmth of the summer), picking gently to prevent tearing

YIELD 13–45kg/30–110lb of fruit per bush tree

GREENFINGER TIP *Don't plant on east- or south-facing walls as this may bring it into flower too early and the blossoms can get caught by frost*

Blackberry
Rubus fruticosus

EASY

'Fantasia'

'Loch Ness'

Blackberries are a prickly cane fruit with pale pink flowers, and are grown for their large, sweet, juicy black berries in late summer and autumn. As a child I used to collect them from the hedgerows for pies and jam, but growing your own makes a bountiful, tasty addition to the menu. Blackberry bushes crop reasonably well even in shady conditions (though more berries are produced in full sun), need very little attention as long as they are planted well, and can crop for up to fifteen years. Only one bush is needed, as they are self-fertile, and are excellent for attracting pollinating insects. However, they are vigorous, growing to 3.5m/12ft, and can get out of hand if not pruned (after all, they are only posh brambles). Most need a support structure of some kind and are usually trained on canes, but can be grown against a fence as a fan, or on pergolas and arches.

VARIETIES 'Bedford Giant' Exceptionally prickly, reliable, high yielding with black juicy fruits (July to August); 'Fantasia' ♧ Vigorous (invasive!), reliable, producing large, sweet berries (August); 'Loch Ness' ♧ Good for small plots, thornless, with medium-sized sweet berries (July to September)

ASPECT Sunny, sheltered site, with protection from winds; tolerant of partial shade

SOIL Fertile, deep, moist, well-drained soil; add well-rotted farmyard manure before planting; pH5.0–7.0

PLANTING Plant container-grown plants all year round as long as ground is not frozen or waterlogged, or plant bare-root specimens in the dormant season from November to March. Space plants 45cm/18in apart. Space rows of larger varieties 4m/13ft apart, medium-sized cultivars 2.5m/8ft and less vigorous growers 1.2m/4ft. Keep the crown of the roots level with soil surface, spreading the roots out into the hole and covering with soil. Water well and trim canes back immediately after planting to about 25cm/10in, to encourage better fruiting the following year (though a bush will only start giving decent yields after two years). Provide supports with posts spaced every 2m/6ft and fix wires between them at 60cm/2ft intervals up to 2m/6ft high, tying in new stems as they grow if training them, or grow as open-centred bushes

CARE Keep crops weed free and water regularly. Protect fruiting bushes from birds with netting. Shoot tips of blackberries root naturally once they come in contact with the soil; dig up and replant

PRUNING Blackberries bear their fruit on one-year-old wood. After harvest, cut the fruited canes down to ground level, leaving those that did not produce berries to fruit next year; tie new canes into the wires as they grow. Repeat this process each year, with new canes replacing old canes to keep the plant productive. Maintain open centres for bushes, removing dead or crossing branches to aid air circulation and protect against mildew

PROBLEMS Aphids; cane spot and downy mildew

HARVESTING Pick berries in July up to October, when they are plump, deep purple to dark black and pull off the bush easily

YIELD 7kg/15lb per bush or 9kg/20lb per 3m/10ft row

Blackcurrant
Ribes nigrum

'Ben Sarek'

Blackcurrants are deciduous bushy plants, with a height and spread of 2m/6ft, which produce attractive, scented, lobed green leaves, and strings of sharp-tasting small, purple-black berries (rich in vitamin C and very popular for jam making). There are earlier and later fruiting varieties so it is possible to have fruit from June through to September. They are largely hardy, but can be damaged by spring frosts. The smaller dwarf varieties grow successfully in pots or containers. Blackcurrants are really easy to grow, but check out any disease-resistant varieties on offer to make life even easier.

VARIETIES 'Ben Hope' Vigorous, tall variety with arguably the best flavoured berries, cropping July to August; good resistance to blackcurrant gall midge, mildew and leaf spot; **'Ben Sarek'** ⚥ Heavy cropping, compact variety (90cm/3ft), bearing black berries on short strings in July; good mildew and frost resistance

ASPECT Sunny or partially shaded site, sheltered from winds and frosts

SOIL Fertile, moist, well-drained soil; apply well-rotted farmyard manure before planting; pH5.4–7.0

PLANTING Plant container-bought bushes all year round as long as ground is not frozen or waterlogged, or plant bare-root plants in November to March. Plant 5cm/2in deeper than in the nursery pot, spacing 1.2–2m/4–6ft between plants and rows. Prune all the stems of newly planted bushes to 2.5cm/1in above soil level immediately after planting; this seems extreme but will help make the bush productive the following year

CARE Mulch the base of the tree with organic matter or grass clippings in spring, to keep weed free and conserve moisture. Water regularly at the base of the plant, avoiding the leaves, and do not let the roots dry out. Increase watering in dry weather, especially when fruits start to swell. Net fruiting bushes to protect from birds. Protect from frost with fleece. Re-pot container-grown bushes every two or three years

PRUNING Blackcurrants fruit on one-year-old wood and do not need pruning in the first winter after planting. In the second and following winters, cut out crossing, diseased, dead or damaged stems and remove any stems crowding the centre; prune one third of the older stems to just above ground level, removing them equally throughout the bush, leaving a mix of young and older wood to keep bushes productive

PROBLEMS Big bud mite, blackcurrant gall midge and capsid bug; American gooseberry mildew and *Botrytis* (grey mould); birds

HARVESTING Pick fruits from July to September, cutting the strings gently with scissors to avoid damaging berries

YIELD 4.5kg/10lb of fruit per bush

BLACKCURRANT GALL MIDGE is a white maggot that feeds on blackcurrant shoot tips, normally spotted with the first flowering of the year. This generation will do most damage as it can reduce the crop; pick maggots off. Grow resistant varieties where possible as there are no chemical controls available to the home gardener.

Blueberry
Vaccinium corymbosum

EASY

'Berkeley'

'Bluecrop'

Blueberries are an increasingly popular soft fruit, rich in antioxidants, and are easy to grow, which is just as well as they are expensive in the shops. They are upright or spreading shrubs, depending on the variety grown, varying in height from dwarf cultivars at 30cm/12in to taller varieties up to 1.5m/5ft. They have attractive pinkish-white flowers that are followed by the delicious, small, inky-black fruits in late summer. New self-fertile varieties are available but some are only partly self-fertile and need more than one variety for a healthy crop. They are versatile, and ideal for pots, hedging and bushes, but they need acid soil and plenty of water to grow and fruit well. Don't expect a worthwhile crop until the third year.

VARIETIES 'Berkeley' Heavy-cropping variety with light blue, sweet berries, ideal for milder areas (plant with another variety); '**Bluecrop**' Good disease resistance, reliable, heavy cropping, with large light blue fruits with sharp flavour in July (partly self-fertile so needs pollinator); '**Spartan**' Heavy cropping, vigorous, with light purple fruits of excellent sweetness in early July (self-fertile)

ASPECT Sunny, sheltered site, with protection from frosts and winds; tolerant of partial shade

SOIL Fertile, light, well-drained, gritty acid soils; not suitable for limey soils; in containers, use ericaceous compost mixed with grit; add organic matter before planting; pH4.0–5.5

PLANTING Plants are usually supplied grown in containers; plant all year round as long as ground is not frozen or waterlogged. Keep the crown of the roots level with the soil surface. Allow 1m/3ft between bushes for compact varieties or 1.5m/5ft for larger bushes

CARE Mulch with organic matter or wood/pine needles (these are acidic) in spring, to keep weed free and conserve moisture. Water regularly with rainwater at the base, and do not let the roots dry out (they are shallow rooted, so dry out easily). Feed with organic fertiliser high in phosphorous or potassium in the early spring. Net fruiting bushes to prevent the birds getting to the fruits before you do. Protect flowers from frost. Re-pot container-grown plants every two to three years in autumn

PRUNING In the first three years, there is no need to prune. In subsequent years, prune after bushes lose their leaves, in February to March, cutting out diseased, dead, weak or damaged stems, aiming for an open centre. Cut a quarter of the total number of stems to 2–3cm/¾–1in above ground level, taking them out evenly through the plant. Cut back twiggy growth at the end of stems that fruited last year to a strong upward-facing bud. Remove two or three unproductive branches each year, cutting to just above ground level in spring

PROBLEMS *Botrytis* (grey mould); birds

HARVESTING Pick berries from August, when they are ripe and dark blue

YIELD 7–9kg /15–20lb per bush

GREENFINGER TIP *Use rainwater for watering, as this is more acidic, and keep soil moist, especially when fruits start to swell*

Cherry, Morello (sour) and Cherry, sweet

Prunus cerasus (Morello cherry)

Prunus avium (sweet cherry)   **EASY**

'Morello'

'Stella'

Cherries belong to the same family as peaches, plums and apricots. Growing them as a tree ensures the most fruit. They are a thing of beauty, with attractive pink to white blossoms in spring. There are two types: the sweet cherry, for eating fresh, and the sour (Morello) cherry, mainly used for cooking, bottling, jams or pies. Morello cherries are largely reliable croppers, tolerate colder and wetter conditions than sweet cherries and are better suited to smaller plots or gardens; grafted dwarf varieties (up to 2m/6ft) are also available. Bear the height in mind when siting them as they will cast shade on other crops. There are some good self-fertile varieties about, but others need pollinators. They fruit over a short season, usually from July. Here's a bit of idle information: the leaves contain minute traces of cyanide!

VARIETIES SOUR CHERRY 'Morello' ☀ Small, heavy-cropping tree with dark red, sharp-tasting fruits from July to August (5m/16ft) (self-fertile) **SWEET CHERRY** 'Stella' ☀ Upright, vigorous, spreading tree with white blossom, generous crops of dark red berries in July (7m/22ft) (self-fertile); 'Summer Sun' ☀ Sturdy tree, heavy cropping, bright cherry-red fruits, good frost tolerance, ripening July to August (3–5m/10–16ft) (self-fertile)

ASPECT Sunny or partially shaded site, sheltered from winds and frosts

SOIL Fertile, rich, moist, well-drained soil; add well-rotted farmyard manure before planting; pH6.5–6.7

PLANTING Plant container-grown trees all year round as long as ground is not frozen or waterlogged, or plant bare-root trees from November to March, spacing 2.5–4m/8–13ft apart for trees and 3.5–5m/12–16ft apart for fans, at least 20cm/8in away from the foot of any wall. Install stakes or wires

CARE Mulch with organic matter round the base in spring. Feed annually with a general fertiliser in late winter. Protect flowers from frost. Protect crops from birds with netting

PRUNING Prune in March for young trees, as the buds break open, and in July and August for mature free-standing trees; never prune in winter as this makes them vulnerable to disease such as silver leaf. For formative pruning, see page 114. Prune established trees lightly, removing any dead, damaged or diseased branches and any crossing or unwanted upright growth, to keep an open centre. Pull, don't cut, any suckers from the base and rub off buds growing on the lower part of the trunk. After harvesting, remove branches that fruited poorly, to stimulate new growth. Paint pruning wounds with a tree sealant

PROBLEMS Aphids, pear and cherry slugworm and winter moth caterpillar; bacterial canker, blossom wilt, silver leaf and *Verticillium* wilt; frost damage, fruit splitting and birds

HARVESTING Harvest ripe fruits when the skin is dark red for jams or cooking, or leave to ripen until nearly black, normally August

YIELD 13–45kg/30–110lb, depending on the form

Fig
Ficus carica

EASY

'Brown Turkey'

White Marseilles'

The smell of a fig tree is enough to transport me to the Mediterranean, yet they do surprisingly well in colder areas. They make a very ornamental, deciduous spreading tree, with large, coarse, deeply lobed leaves and large, tear-drop-shaped, seeded sweet fruits from August to September. They can be grown as free-standing trees and do well as fans against a warm wall. Figs need their roots restricted to crop well: growing them in pots will provide the necessary root restriction. The sap is a skin irritant.

VARIETIES 'Brown Turkey' ℧ Reliable, heavy-cropping variety with reddy-brown skins and sweet pink flesh; **'White Marseilles'** September-ripening, heavy-cropping variety with green skins and green sweet flesh

ASPECT Sunny, sheltered site, with protection from winds; or on a south-west-facing wall

SOIL Fertile, well-drained soil; pH6.0–7.8

PLANTING Plant container-grown plants from November to March. Line the planting hole with paving slabs and fill the base with rubble to restrict the root run, or plant in a large container (30–40cm/12–16in diameter); plant slightly deeper than the container they came in. Install stakes or horizontal wires, spaced 45cm/18in apart. Keep well watered until established

CARE Mulch the base with well-rotted manure; in spring apply a high-potash feed (such as tomato fertiliser) weekly when fruit begins to swell; water regularly

PRUNING Pruning almost doubles the amount of fruits, but you can do absolutely nothing and still have a fairly respectable crop. For formative pruning (in March), see page 114. Prune established trees and fans from March to April, once frost risk has passed, removing dead, diseased or damaged material, any buds or shoots that face inwards and any upright growth crowding the centre. Every three or four years, remove an old unproductive branch to encourage new productive growth. Prune again in June, shortening side shoots back to five leaves from the main branch framework. Baby or embryo figs develop in the leaf axils in late summer and will overwinter to mature into ripe figs next year, when a new crop will again be produced. Pull off figs formed earlier in the year, though, as these are unlikely to ripen before autumn, to allow the developing figs to grow larger for next year

PROBLEMS Brown scale and red spider mite; frost damage, birds and wasps

HARVESTING Pick figs as they ripen: they droop on the stalk, the skins deepen in colour and often split. Net the tree or pick ripe figs immediately or the birds and wasps will beat you to it

YIELD 2–9kg/4–20lb from a mature plant

GREENFINGER TIP *An old boy on an allotment told me that if you dip a clean needle into olive oil and then slide it into the eye of a fig, it will ripen more quickly. I don't understand the science behind this idea, but it works*

Gooseberry
Ribes uva-crispa

'Leveller'

'Whinham's Industry'

Gooseberries are spreading or upright bushes, with a height of 90cm/3ft and spread of 1.5m/5ft. They have sharp thorns and rounded, hairy, fleshy berries, that are usually green but can also be red or white; both dessert and cooking varieties are available. Normally grown as bushes, they can be trained against walls or grown in pots or containers, and may fruit for up to twenty years. They are all self-fertile, so only one bush is needed to produce fruit. They are one of the most delicious soft fruits – a ripe gooseberry is a thing of wonder. Many plants will put up with light shade, and will do for cooler areas, so this is a great crop for northern gardeners. They are easy to grow but do attract mildew, so check out any mildew-resistant varieties before purchasing.

VARIETIES 'Invicta' ☸ Compact, prickly and heavy cropping, with tasty pale green fruits from July to August; good for container growing; mildew resistant; **'Leveller'** ☸ Very popular, with excellent-flavoured, large, oval, pale green berries; **'Whinham's Industry'** ☸ Delicious red berries, vigorous and shade tolerant

ASPECT Sunny, sheltered site, with protection from frosts and winds; tolerant of light shade

SOIL Fertile, moist, well-drained soil; add well-rotted manure or organic matter before planting; pH5.5–6.5

PLANTING Plant container-grown bushes all year round as long as ground is not frozen or waterlogged (planting to the same depth as in the pot), or plant bare-root plants from November to March, spacing 1.2–1.5m/4–5ft between plants and rows

CARE Apply a general fertiliser in March and then mulch base with organic matter. Water regularly, especially when the fruit starts swelling. Net crops from winter onwards to protect fruit and buds from foraging birds. Pull, don't cut, any suckers from the base of the plant in winter

PRUNING Prune in February each year, aiming for a goblet shape with an open centre to ensure plenty of light and air circulation, as this helps prevent mildew: cut out any weak, diseased or dead branches and any growth in the centre of the bush. Always prune to an outward-facing bud for upright bushes and an upward-facing bud for spreading varieties. Cut old, long side shoots to 2.5cm/1in from the base and leave all young growth untouched

PROBLEMS Aphids, capsid bug, caterpillars and gooseberry sawfly; American gooseberry mildew and *Botrytis* (grey mould); birds and squirrels

HARVESTING Pick small, pea-sized gooseberries from late May to June to use for cooking, leaving the rest to ripen and grow larger for harvesting from July

YIELD 4.5kg/10lb of fruit per bush

Grape
Vitis vinifera

'Boskoop Glory'

'Schiava Grossa'

Grape vines are vigorous, deciduous climbers grown as much for their ornamental appeal in the garden as their fruits. Grapes are a high-maintenance crop, needing regular training and pruning, and are entirely reliant on long, hot summers and warm, dry autumns to crop well (good drainage is also essential). So think carefully before deciding to grow them, ensuring you have the right site for them, and enough time and space. If you are in a cold, northerly region, choose an early-ripening variety.

VARIETIES 'Boskoop Glory' ♀ Reliably cropping, loose bunches of sweet black grapes; suitable outdoors; 'Brandt' ♀ Heavy cropping, small, purple, sweet dessert grapes; 'Buckland Sweetwater' Compact, with sweet, small white grapes, better suited to indoor growing; 'Schiava Grossa' (also known as 'Black Hamburgh') Large, sweet, plump, dark purple grapes; better suited to indoor growing

ASPECT Sunny, sheltered site, with protection from winds and frosts, against a south or south-west wall; or in a greenhouse

SOIL Fertile, humus-rich, well-drained soil; pH5.5–6.8

PLANTING Plant container-grown plants indoors from November to March in pots in a conservatory or in a greenhouse bed. (Alternatively, if you are growing the vine in a greenhouse, plant the vine outside in March, in the soil next to the greenhouse, make a hole in the wall and train the trunk to grow inside; this will cut down the need for watering and makes feeding easier.) Plant outdoors in March, on a warm wall facing south or south-west, adding well-rotted manure to the planting hole; install five or six horizontal wires, about 30cm/12in apart to just above head height, using vine eyes

CARE Grapes grown outdoors: mulch the base with organic matter in February, but ensure the manure does not make contact with the stem; feed once with a potash fertiliser when grape bunches have formed and fruits begin to colour up. **Grapes grown indoors**: most vines will do well in an unheated greenhouse, though a boost of heat in February in colder areas will help; try to maintain a minimum night temperature of 4–7°C/39–45°F. If the vine is growing in a constantly heated greenhouse or conservatory in winter, open vents or a window for ventilation, to lower the risk of *Botrytis* (grey mould) and ensure that humidity levels are reduced as the fruits ripen. Ventilation is very important, as fungal infections thrive in cramped, humid conditions. Feed indoor plants with a high-potash feed, from about a month after growth begins until the grapes start to swell. Water regularly if the roots are planted indoors; if the vine is planted outside and trained into the greenhouse, it will need very little

Grape (continued)

'Buckland Sweetwater'

watering once established, except in very dry weather. From December to January, peel away loose bark to reveal mealybug or brown scale and spray with a winter wash. **For all grapes**: if too much fruit is allowed to develop, *Botrytis* (grey mould) sets in. Once the vine is established, from year three, thin each bunch of grapes by two thirds to allow them to grow to a good size and help avoid this. Cut out bunches of grapes that fall too near each other with a small pair of pointed scissors to allow space between bunches. Avoid handling the remaining grapes. Use a copper-based fungicide such as Bordeaux mixture to help combat fungal disease or grow disease-resistant varieties, where possible. Remove any large leaves that shade the grape bunches

PRUNING Train indoor and outdoor vines in the same way (see right). The horizontal wires will support the side shoots (laterals) that produce the fruit, with the main stem (leader) growing vertically. In the first three years, the aim is to grow a strong framework, so don't allow fruit to develop for the first two years. Grapes form on new wood, so repeat the third-year pruning annually for fruiting

PROBLEMS Aphids and brown scale; *Botrytis* (grey mould) and downy mildew; frost damage, birds and wasps

HARVESTING Pick bunches of grapes by snipping with scissors once the grapes are sweet to taste, from September

YIELD 10 bunches per vine

Training grape vines

FORMATIVE PRUNING

YEAR ONE In January, prune to within two buds of the base. When buds start growing in spring, tie the single main growing shoot (the leader) vertically to the wires and train up a cane for support; shorten any side shoots to 2.5cm/1in

YEAR TWO In November to December, prune the leader down to half and prune side shoots again to 2.5cm/1in

YEAR THREE In spring select two or more strong side shoots and allow these to develop, tying them in loosely to horizontal wires: one right and one left of the main stem. From November to December, shorten these to 60cm/2ft from the main stem

ESTABLISHED PRUNING

After Year Three, the vine is established and you can increase the number of bunches you grow. After winter pruning, decide how many buds you will allow to develop. Allow the allocated buds to produce side shoots that you tie in to the horizontal wires in spring when they are still easily pliable. Tie each on left and right again, each year building up tiers at right angles to the main stem. In summer, prune fruiting laterals to two leaves beyond the fruit and cut back all non-fruiting laterals to five leaves

Hazel

Corylus avellana (cobnut) and *Corylus maxima* (filbert)

EASY

'Kentish Cob'

'Purpurea'

This deciduous tree is a common sight in countryside and hedgerows, with its bare winter branches dangling with catkins and the fresh green heart-shaped leaves appearing from spring. No doubt you have gathered a pocketful of the sweet white nuts on autumn walks without even thinking of growing one yourself, but hazels are very easy to look after and well worth it if you have the space. Fruiting will be better if you plant two varieties, one as a pollinator. As in all trees that are wind pollinated, yields can be variable. If you are short of space, some nurseries sell twin trees, with two compatible varieties grafted on to one stem, so the guesswork is taken out of the equation.

VARIETIES COBNUT **'Pearson's Prolific'** (formerly 'Nottingham Prolific') Compact, with small, sweet-tasting nuts; good pollinator (3m/10ft × 4m/13ft) **FILBERT 'Kentish Cob'** Upright, vigorous English variety, heavy crops of larger, long-shaped sweet nuts; good pollinator (5m/16ft); **'Purpurea'** 🏆 Very ornamental purple-leaved variety, with purple catkins and small nuts with fabulous flavour, best grown as a bush for better cropping (3m/10ft × 4m/13ft)

ASPECT Sunny, sheltered site, with protection from frost and winds; tolerant of partial shade

SOIL Fertile, well-drained soil; pH5.5–6.0

PLANTING Plant container-grown trees all year round as long as soil is not frozen or waterlogged, or plant bare-root trees in mid-October; bare-root specimens establish more quickly. Stake young trees

CARE Mulch the base of the tree in spring with garden compost to preserve moisture and prevent weeds

PRUNING For formative pruning, see page 114; leave about eight branches to form the framework, for good cropping. Prune established trees in December to February, remove dead, diseased or damaged material and any upright growth in the centre, to maintain an open shape; remove one or two of the older stems every year. Pull, don't cut, suckers growing from the base. If the tree has been coppiced in the past, coppice (cut some or all stems to the ground) every seven to ten years; use cut stems as plant supports

PROBLEMS Nut weevil; powdery mildew; squirrels

HARVESTING Let nuts fall to the ground in autumn and collect them

YIELD 15kg/33lb from a mature tree, considerably less in younger trees

NUT WEEVIL is commonly found in filberts and cobnuts. The grubs tunnel their way out around August, eating the white nut and leaving small holes in the shells. This only affects a small amount of the crop. There are no effective measures, so look before you bite!

GREENFINGER TIP *Planting bush trees in a square formation will greatly assist with pollination and give more generous yields*

Loganberry and Tayberry

Rubus × loganobaccus (loganberry)

Rubus Tayberry Group (tayberry)   **EASY**

'Ly 59'

'Buckingham'

Cross the American dewberry with a raspberry and the result is a loganberry: a trailing plant with long, dark-wine-coloured, juicy, slightly sharp-tasting fruits. The varieties available are limited: thorny or non-thorny is the choice, so it depends how much punishment you can bear when it comes to harvest time. The tayberry is a cross between a blackberry and a raspberry and has long, dark reddish purple, juicy, sharp-tasting fruits. Both are certainly worth growing as they are simply delicious and need so little pruning that they are an ideal crop for the novice.

VARIETIES LOGANBERRY 'Ly 59' ⚥ Vigorous, very thorny, with long, acidic berries; 'Ly 654' ⚥ Moderately vigorous, thornless, with sweet red fruits **TAYBERRY** 'Buckingham' Thornless, with large, reddish-black, juicy fruits (about 5cm/2in long), cropping summer to autumn

ASPECT Cool, shady site, with protection from frosts and winds

SOIL Fertile, moist, well-drained soil; add well-rotted manure or organic matter before planting; pH6.0–7.0

PLANTING Plant container-grown bushes all year round as long as ground is not frozen or waterlogged, or plant bare-root plants in November to March. Allow 45cm/18in between plants. Space rows of large vigorous cultivars 4m/13ft apart; medium growers 2.5m/8ft apart and more compact varieties 1.2m/4ft apart. Cover the roots with about 8cm/3in of soil, firm soil and water well. Cut newly planted canes to 23cm/9in above ground level after planting to encourage strong root growth for fruiting the following year

CARE Loganberries and tayberries need support; grow along a fence or tie to garden wire fixed tautly between two or more strong stakes (this method will ensure adequate airflow around the plant and help prevent fungal disease); tie in new canes as they grow. To propagate, dig up newly formed canes and their rootballs intact, cut them away from the main row and replant in situ

PRUNING After harvest, cut the fruited canes to the base; remove any weak shoots or canes that are growing out of line but don't cut back any canes that have not fruited as they will bear fruit next year

PROBLEMS Aphids; raspberry beetle

HARVESTING Pick little and often to encourage more fruit. Fruit is ripe when the berries are dark, plump and juicy. If in doubt, taste them! They ripen steadily from July to October for immediate use or to be stored by freezing

YIELD 3.5kg/8lb per bush

Medlar
Mespilus germanica

EASY

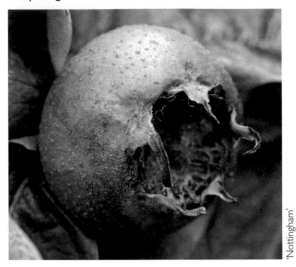

'Nottingham'

Medlar blossom

The medlar is the most beautiful deciduous tree, which has been grown in the UK since the sixteenth century. It has a mounded shape and pretty, single, white flowers in May to June and attractive russet-coloured leaves in autumn. Trees reach 4m/13ft × 3m/10ft in ten years and are grown not only for their hugely ornamental features but also for the rather unusual, seeded brown fruits. These taste dreadful until after they start to rot (known as bletting), when the sharp acidic taste mellows to a honeyed sweetness and they are traditionally used for preserves and jelly making. A medlar will take some years to develop, but buying a two-year-old tree will give you a bit of a head start, and it can live for sixty years or more, so you will have the pleasure of this beautiful tree for life.

VARIETIES 'Nottingham' Compact, with slightly weeping habit, fruits November–December (self-fertile); 'Royal' Popular Dutch variety, very sweet fruits; 'Westerveld' Earlier cropping (October)

ASPECT Sunny, sheltered site, with protection from winds; tolerant of light shade

SOIL Fertile, well-drained soil; pH6.0–7.8

PLANTING Plant container-grown trees all year round as long as soil is not frozen or waterlogged, or plant bare-root trees from November to March. Stake young trees

CARE Mulch the base with organic matter in winter to keep down weeds and preserve moisture; water well for the first four or five years, while establishing, after which there is no need to water

PRUNING For formative pruning, see page 114. Once the framework is established they rarely need further pruning, other than to remove any dead, diseased or damaged wood

PROBLEMS Aphids and caterpillars; powdery mildew

HARVESTING Pick ripe fruits as late as possible in October to November and store in a box in a cool, dry place until they turn a dark reddy brown and become soft and juicy – normally after two to three weeks

YIELD 13–27kg/30–60lb of fruit from a mature tree

GREENFINGER TIP *To blet medlars indoors, dip the stalks in diluted salt water (which prevents fruit rot) and place the unripe fruit with the eye facing downwards. They should turn brown and be ready for eating after a few weeks*

Mulberry, black
Morus nigra ♀

EASY

'Chelsea'

Unripened fruits

This beautiful, spreading, deciduous tree with fresh green, toothed, heart-shaped leaves which turn yellow in autumn is slow growing but can reach an ultimate height of 6m/20ft. The delicious dark purple fruits, a little like raspberries, ripen over some weeks to produce the unique, sharp taste from July to August (beware: the juice stains like mad). They are self-fertile, and the hardest thing about growing a mulberry is getting to the fruits before the birds. Trees need to be at least five years old before they fruit and then crops are unpredictable, but you must forgive this in such a handsome tree with such rare-flavoured fruit. On the plus side, they tolerate a wide range of soils, provided they have good drainage. If you want a beautiful tree for the kitchen garden or allotment, this is it – but you will need the space to let it grow unfettered.

VARIETIES 'Chelsea' Old variety, with delicious, large red fruits of great flavour, excellent for eating fresh, for preserves and gin-making, cropping August (3m/10ft × 4m/13ft after ten years)

ASPECT Very warm, sunny site, with protection from frosts and wind

SOIL Fertile, moist, well-drained, sandy loam soil; add well-rotted manure or organic matter before planting; pH5.0–5.7

PLANTING Plant container-grown trees all year round as long as ground is not frozen or waterlogged, or plant bare-root trees from November to March. Stake young trees

CARE The flowers are rarely at risk from frosts as mulberries flower late in summer. Give extra water in extended dry periods in the first four years from planting. Apply organic mulch or garden compost at the base of the tree in spring to conserve moisture to the roots and keep weeds down

PRUNING For formative pruning, see page 114. Prune only in December or January when the tree is dormant, otherwise the sap bleeds. Both young and established trees need very little pruning: just remove dead, diseased, damaged or crossing wood

PROBLEMS Canker; birds

HARVESTING Fruits ripen over several weeks, not all at once; pick the darkened fruits from July to August or harvest paler fruits for preserves earlier

YIELD 2.5kg/4–5lb from a mature tree

GREENFINGER TIP *Large trees are impractical to pick and the fruits splat to the ground if you don't keep popping out to check whether they are ripe, so lay a plastic sheet on the ground to catch the ripened fruit as it drops*

Peach and Nectarine
Prunus persica (peach)

'Peregrine'

Prunus persica var. nectarina (nectarine)   **TRICKY**

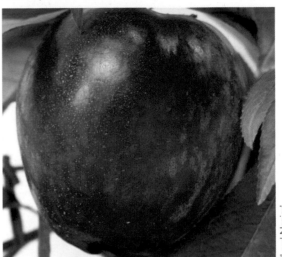

'Lord Napier'

Peaches and nectarines are small, fairly fast-growing, but relatively short-lived deciduous trees bearing attractive pale pink blossoms with carmine stamens in spring, and mouth-watering fruits. Nectarines have smooth, warm, red-orange skins, whereas peaches have soft, felty skins of pale apricot. Both are cared for in much the same manner: grow in warm, sheltered areas or against a south-facing wall (they can be fan trained). They flower early, when there are few pollinating insects about, so the blossom will need protection and it may be necessary to hand pollinate them. They will do well in large containers or pots as long as shelter is provided and patio peaches are available for small spaces. All, without fail, need long, hot, dry summers to produce a worthwhile crop.

VARIETIES PEACH 'Bonanza' Dwarf, ideal for pots, with pale apricot-yellow fruits in July (1.5m/5ft × 1.5m/5ft) (self-fertile); 'Peregrine' ♀ Popular, with flushed pink skin, juicy fruit in August (4.5m/15ft × 4.5m/15ft) (self-fertile) **NECTARINE** 'Early Rivers' ♀ Sweet flesh and pale yellow skin flushed pink in July (3.5m/12ft × 3.5m/12ft); 'Lord Napier' ♀ Ideal for fans or bush training, with large, juicy fruit in August (3.5–4.5m/12–15ft) (self-fertile)

ASPECT Very warm, sunny, sheltered site, with protection from frosts and wind; not recommended as free-standing trees in cooler areas

SOIL Fertile, well-drained, deep loam soil; add well-rotted manure or organic matter before planting; pH6.0–7.0

PLANTING Plant container-grown plants all year round as long as ground is not frozen or waterlogged, or plant bare-root trees from October to November. Stake young trees or install wires if growing as a fan

CARE Mulch well in spring with organic matter. Protect blossom from frosts with fleece. Give wall-trained plants a high-potash feed or tomato fertiliser at fortnightly intervals once fruits are formed until harvest

PRUNING For formative pruning of free-standing trees, in March, see page 114. Prune young fans in March, tying in branches to fan-shaped canes and cutting back each branch by about one third to a healthy bud. Prune established trees and fans from June to July, removing any diseased, damaged or weak growth. If the tree bears lots of small fruitlets (the size of a hazelnut), thin by removing every other fruitlet, leaving the rest about 5cm/2in apart. Thin again once they swell to the size of a walnut, to 15cm/6in apart

PROBLEMS Aphids; blossom wilt, cankers, peach leaf curl and silver leaf; frost damage and birds

HARVESTING Harvest from July to September, when the flesh near the stalk gives slightly when pressed and the fruit parts from the tree easily

YIELD 20kg/44lb per mature tree

PEACH LEAF CURL is a fungal disease that overwinters in the bark, attacking young leaves and flowers, so that fruit fail to form. Treat with Bordeaux mixture in January and again in February if necessary to kill the fungus. Remove all fruit from the tree as they will never grow properly. Mulch the base well and apply a nitrogen-rich fertiliser, watering in well.

Pear
Pyrus communis

'Conference'

'Doyenné du Comice'

Pears are attractive, upright, mainly deciduous trees bearing white blossoms. They are slightly more fussy than apples, and need warmth and plenty of sun to crop well. They can grow to 17m/55ft tall, though grafted stock allows more compact varieties to be grown, and may live up to 200 years, so make sure you plant them in the right place. They can be grown as free-standing trees, fans, espaliers or cordons, but varieties that crop at the tips (known as tip bearers) should be grown as bush-type trees. Disease resistance differs with varieties, as does tolerance to cold and windy conditions. Some pears are self-fertile, but many varieties will need another tree nearby, as a pollinator, to bear good fruit crops. If unsure, seek the advice of a good fruit nursery.

VARIETIES 'Beurré Hardy' ⚥ Heavy cropping, with red russeted fruit in October; suitable for eating and cooking; will do well in cooler regions (9m/30ft × 8m/26ft); **'Conference'** ⚥ Reliable eating variety, cropping October to November (6m/20ft × 6m/20ft) (partially self-fertile); **'Doyenné du Comice'** ⚥ Dessert variety, large golden fruits with lightly russeted skins, from November to December; fruits store well (pollinator 'Concorde' required) (9m/30ft × 8m/26ft); **'Williams Bon Chrétien'** ⚥ Well-known earlier variety, pale yellow, delicious juicy fruits in September (5m/16ft × 5m/16ft)

ASPECT Very warm, sunny site, with protection from frosts and wind; not recommended as a free-standing tree in cooler areas

SOIL Fertile, well-drained soil; add well-rotted manure or organic matter before planting; pears may struggle on thin, light or hungry soils; pH6.0–7.0

PLANTING Plant container-grown plants all year round as long as ground is not frozen or waterlogged, or plant bare-root trees from November to March. Space larger trees 10m/32ft apart, dwarf trees 6m/20ft apart. Stake young trees or install wires if growing as a fan

CARE Mulch well in spring with organic matter or garden compost at the base of the tree to preserve moisture and help suppress weeds. Do not allow tree roots to dry out, even when mature

PRUNING For formative pruning, see page 114. Prune established trees in winter, removing dead, diseased or damaged branches. Pears bear more fruit than the branches can cope with (leading to a natural fall of immature fruit, known as June drop), so thin fruit after this every year. Remove fruit by hand, leaving one per cluster, spacing clusters 15cm/6in apart; start at one end of a branch and work along

PROBLEMS Capsid bug, caterpillars, codling moth, pear and cherry slugworm; apple powdery mildew, blossom wilt, cankers, scab, *Verticillium* wilt; frost damage and birds

HARVESTING Harvesting at exactly the right moment can be a bit hit and miss: pick too early and the fruits are hard, dry and bland, pick too late and they are overripe. Pears can ripen so rapidly that it is best to pick one or two fruits over a number of days until you find the ideal consistency

YIELD 18kg/40lb from a tree

Plum, Greengage, Bullace and Damson

Prunus domestica (plum)

'Marjorie's Seedling'

Prunus domestica (greengage)   **EASY**

'Imperial Gage'

Plums are upright, small to medium-sized deciduous trees with oval leaves and small white flowers from April to May. They produce fleshy, juicy, oval fruit and the skins can be red, yellow and purple. Greengages are similar, but are sturdier bushy trees and not so hardy; the rounded, yellow-green fruits are smaller than plums. Greengages can be difficult to grow as they crop erratically, needing long cold winters to fruit well, but the fruit is, in my humble opinion, infinitely superior. Most plums and greengages are self-fertile, but crop better if grown with another plum for pollination.

VARIETIES PLUM 'Jubilee' Reliable, hardy, with large reddish plums and sweet yellow flesh; excellent disease resistance (3–4m/10–13ft) (self-fertile); **'Marjorie's Seedling'** ☸ Heavy cropping, with large, oval, deep purple-black fruits and juicy yellow flesh in autumn (5m/16ft × 5m/16ft) (self-fertile) GREENGAGE **'Imperial Gage'** ☸ Heavy cropping, large, pale green fruits with sweet flavour in mid-summer (5m/16ft × 5m/16ft) (self-fertile: good pollinator); **'Early Transparent Gage'** Heavy cropping, with pale yellow fruits, speckled red in late summer (4m/13ft × 4m/13ft) (self-fertile)

ASPECT Sunny, sheltered site, with protection from frosts and winds

SOIL Fertile, moist, well-drained soil; add organic matter or leafmould before planting; pH5.5–6.5

PLANTING To get a head start, choose a three-year-old tree with a good branch framework. Plant container-grown trees all year round as long as ground is not frozen or waterlogged, or plant bare-root trees from November to March. Space 4m/13ft apart for bush trees and fans, and 7.5m/25ft apart for standard trees. Stake young trees or install wires if growing against a warm wall

CARE Mulch the base of plants in spring with garden compost to keep weed free and preserve moisture. Water young trees regularly while establishing, particularly in dry periods. Protect flowers from frost damage as this will affect fruit production. Apply bonemeal in spring or autumn and water in thoroughly

PRUNING For formative pruning, see page 114. Once established, prune every two to five years in June or July, never winter, to prevent the tree falling prey to silver leaf. Remove dead or damaged branches and keep an open centre by cutting out crossed and congested branches. Seal large wounds with beeswax or a protective sealer

PROBLEMS Caterpillars and plum sawfly; blossom wilt, silver leaf and *Verticillium* wilt; birds and wasps

HARVESTING Plums can be picked many times over during the harvesting season from August and give the best flavour if left to ripen on the tree. When ripe they should be firm, but give a little when pressed; alternatively, taste one. Pick greengage when ripe from August to September for immediate use or pick hard, green fruits for longer storage

Plum, Greengage, Bullace and Damson (continued)

Prunus insititia (bullace)

Prunus insititia (damson)

Bullace

'Merryweather Damson'

Bullace and damsons belong to the plum family. Bullace are really wild plums, more commonly seen with their white spring blossoms growing in hedgerows. They crop more heavily than plums, bearing prolific quantities of rounded, stoned black fruit with yellow flesh in September or October that are used for cooking. Damsons produce their pretty white flowers a little later, in April, and bear oval, drooping, acidic, purple-black, stoned fruits, ripening in September. These are traditionally used for jam making; the ripe fruits, though sharper than a plum, are undeniably delicious. They are both self-fertile and rarely grow to more than 5m/16ft, making them a good choice for smaller spaces.

VARIETIES BULLACE 'Langley Bullace' Heavy cropping, with large, dusky, black fruit with greenish-yellow flesh in autumn (4–4.5m/13–15ft); **'Yellow Apricot'** Large, pale yellow, sharp-tasting fruits in early autumn (4–4.5m/13–15ft) DAMSON 'Merryweather Damson' Large, flavoursome, dusky, blue-black fruits in autumn, good for exposed and wet conditions; **'Prune Damson'** ♀ Compact, with blue-black fruits with greenish yellow flesh and acutely sharp flavour in autumn (4m/13ft × 5m/16ft)

ASPECT Sunny, sheltered site, with protection from frosts and winds

SOIL Fertile, moist, well-drained soil; add organic matter or leafmould before planting; pH5.5–6.5

PLANTING To get a head start, choose a three-year-old tree with a good branch framework. Plant container-grown trees all year round as long as ground is not frozen or waterlogged, or plant bare-root trees from November to March. Space 4m/13ft apart for bush trees and fans, and 7.5m/25ft apart for standard trees. Stake young trees or install wires if growing against a warm wall

CARE Mulch the base of plants in spring with garden compost to keep weed free and preserve moisture. Water young trees regularly while establishing, particularly in dry periods. Protect flowers from frost damage as this will affect fruit production. Apply bonemeal in spring or autumn and water in thoroughly

PRUNING For formative pruning, see page 114. Once established, prune every two to five years in June or July, never winter, to prevent the tree falling prey to silver leaf. Remove dead or damaged branches and keep an open centre by cutting out crossed and congested branches. Seal large wounds with beeswax or a protective sealer

PROBLEMS Caterpillars and plum sawfly; blossom wilt, silver leaf and *Verticillium* wilt; birds and wasps

HARVESTING Pick damsons and bullace in autumn, when they are firm but juicy and pull away from the stem easily

GREENFINGER TIP *Pruned bullace (as opposed to wild bullace) has nasty thorns: wear gloves when picking fruit*

Quince
Cydonia oblonga

EASY

Quince blossom

'Vranja'

Belonging to the pear family, quince is a highly ornamental shrub or small tree (with height and spread of 5m/16ft) and can be grown free-standing or trained as a fan on a warm wall. It is multi-stemmed, with large, pinkish white flowers in spring and large, fragrant, pear-shaped fruits from September to November. These are traditionally used to make jellies, jams and quince cheese, as the fruits don't have a long enough season in the UK to ripen fully and be eaten fresh. They do well in most soils and in coastal areas too. A friend has grown one very successfully in a large pot, so there is no reason why gardeners with small spaces shouldn't grow them in good-sized containers.

VARIETIES 'Meech's Prolific' American variety with golden-yellow fruits, cropping early (4m/13ft × 4m/13ft) (self-fertile); 'Vranja' ⅋ Fragrant golden fruits (4m/13ft × 4m/13ft) (self-fertile)

ASPECT Sunny, sheltered site, with protection from winds and frosts; train against a south- or south-west-facing wall in colder areas

SOIL Fertile, moist, well-drained soil; pH6.0–7.0

PLANTING For a head start, choose a two-year-old tree with the branch framework already established. Plant container-grown plants all year round as long as ground is not frozen or waterlogged, or plant bare-root trees from November to March. Stake young trees or install wires, depending on what form you have decided to grow

CARE Keep well watered until established, and mulch in the first few years to prevent roots drying out

PRUNING For formative pruning, see page 114. Once established, prune from November to March to keep an open centre or reduce overcrowding, removing dead, diseased, damaged or crossing branches

PROBLEMS Codling moth and pear and cherry slugworm; apple powdery mildew, fireblight, quince leaf blight and *Verticillium* wilt; frost damage

HARVESTING Harvest in October to November before the fruit falls to the ground and store in a cool, airy place

YIELD 45kg/100lb per mature tree

GREENFINGER TIP *Quince leaf blight is a fungal infection causing brown blotches on the leaves and fruits, and often leading to leaves dropping prematurely. Prune out all infected plant material, pick up any fallen debris and burn*

Raspberry
Rubus idaeus

EASY

'Malling Jewel'

Ranking up there amongst the best of all summer berries (and my favourite certainly), raspberries are soft fruits with lustrous, deep pinky-red berries. They are grown on canes, reaching 1.5–2m/5–6ft × 30–60cm/12–24in. Most fruit in summer and grow well in colder areas; those that fruit in autumn, right up to the first frosts, are a mouth-watering soft red or soft gold, depending on the variety, and normally do better in warmer regions: it is lovely to have a succession of fruit from summer through to autumn. They are easy to grow and can fruit for up to fifteen years, so are a really worthwhile investment, and you can pack a fair amount of fruit production into a relatively small area.

VARIETIES SUMMER 'Glen Moy' ♛ Spineless, large, sweet fruits with good aphid resistance; **'Malling Jewel'** ♛ Popular, reliable, compact, with good virus resistance AUTUMN 'Autumn Bliss' ♛ Heavier cropping than many autumn varieties, ripening from August to first frosts; 'Fallgold' Deliciously sweet, pale golden

ASPECT Sunny, sheltered site; tolerant of partial shade in mild areas

SOIL Fertile, moist, well-drained soil; add well-rotted farmyard manure or organic matter before planting; pH4.5–7.0

PLANTING Plant container-grown plants all year round as long as ground is not frozen or waterlogged, but canes establish best from November to March. Plant deeper than the nursery pot by 5–8cm/2–3in and immediately cut off 20–30cm/8–12in of the top growth

to help prevent the effects of raspberry cane midge. Space plants at 45cm/18in apart along a row, with 1.5–2m/5–6ft between rows for summer-fruiting varieties, 2m/6ft for autumn fruiting. Raspberries need posts (spaced 3m/10ft apart) and horizontal wire supports (45cm/18in apart)

CARE Mulch plants with organic matter at the base in spring, to preserve moisture and keep weeds down. Tie in stems as they grow. Water well, especially in dry weather and once the fruits start to form. To propagate, dig up newly formed canes and their rootballs intact, cut them away from the main row and replant in situ

PRUNING For summer-fruiting varieties, allow five to seven canes to fruit in the first year; cut all canes that have fruited down to just above ground level after fruiting in autumn; select the strongest new canes and tie these into the support wires, cutting the tops of the canes to 15cm/6in above the top wire; any canes that are growing out of line should also be cut down to ground level. For autumn-fruiting varieties, cut all the canes to ground level in March: the crop is carried on new canes, produced during the summer

PROBLEMS Aphids and raspberry beetle; cane spot

HARVESTING Pick ripe berries gently (to prevent squashing) when they are slightly soft but firm and sweet tasting, from July to October

YIELD 3kg/6–7lb per 90cm/3ft row for summer varieties; 1kg/2lb per 90cm/3ft row for autumn-fruiting cultivars

Red and white currants

Ribes rubrum (redcurrants)

'Red Lake'

Ribes rubrum (whitecurrants) **EASY**

'Versailles Blanche'

Redcurrants and the less widely grown white-currants are shrubby, deciduous bushes that have fresh green ornamental leaves and bear long strings of sharp-tasting, vivid red berries, or white berries that mature to creamy yellow when ripe. The berries are not only delicious but good for you too, crammed with vitamin C and antioxidants. Bushes can reach up to 1.5–2m/5–6ft × 90cm/3ft in ideal conditions, and more compact forms are available. They are easy-peasy to grow: they are self-fertile, so there are no worries about pollination, very hardy and will put up with poorer soil than almost all other fruits. Normally grown as free-standing bushes, they can also be trained on a short leg as an espalier, fan or cordon. Check for disease-resistant varieties when purchasing.

VARIETIES RED 'Jonkheer van Tets' ☸ Vigorous, with vivid red fruits in mid-summer, ideal for pies, jellies and jam making; **'Red Lake'** ☸ Brilliant, large, juicy red berries in mid-summer WHITE 'White Pearl' Compact, with sweet, translucent, pale golden berries in mid-summer (90–120cm/3–4ft); **'Versailles Blanche'** Reliable, vigorous, upright, with sweet white currants and good disease resistance

ASPECT Full sun or partial shade (plants in shade will crop later and bear less fruit), with protection from frosts and wind

SOIL Fertile, moist, well-drained soil; add well-rotted manure or organic matter before planting; will tolerate poorer soils as long as well drained; pH6.0–7.0

PLANTING Plant container-grown plants all year round as long as ground is not frozen or waterlogged, or plant bare-root plants when the plant is dormant from November to March, spacing bushes 1.4m/4½ft apart and 1.5m/5ft between rows; space single cordons 45cm/18in apart. Install supports and wires for cordons and fans

CARE Mulch with organic matter at the base of plants in spring and apply a high-potash feed at the start of the growing season. Water regularly, especially in dry weather and when the fruits start to swell. Keep weed free and pull out any suckering shoots that come from the base. Once the harvest is over, there is no need to water until the start of the next growing season

PRUNING Cut stems to 20–30cm/8–12in immediately after planting. Prune established red and whitecurrants from February to early March. Remove dead, damaged or diseased wood to keep an open centre and maximise air circulation and light to the bush, as this will minimise the risk of *Botrytis* (grey mould). Fruit is borne on two- to three-year-old wood, so remove up to one third of older wood from the base of the plant each year, and shorten any leggy stems; leaving a mix of new and older wood keeps the bush productive

PROBLEMS Aphids and capsid bug; *Botrytis* (grey mould); birds

HARVESTING Pick fruit in strings, not individually, from July to August, when ripe

YIELD 4kg/9lb per bush for both red and white currants

FRUIT

Rhubarb
Rheum × hybridum

'Hawke's Champagne'

Harvesting rhubarb

Rhubarb is a hardy perennial that is technically a vegetable, with thick woody rhizomes and long wands of delicious, pinky red and green leaf stalks with large green leaves, growing up to 90cm/3ft in height and spread. It is a very ornamental plant and is usually grown from crowns. Undemanding and easy to grow (I have seen it growing quite happily on allotment compost heaps), it does need plenty of space and individual plants are productive for five to ten years. It can be forced for early cropping and by choosing different varieties it is possible to have a crop from May to August.

VARIETIES 'Cawood Delight' Deep red, good for outdoor cropping, not suitable for forcing; 'Hawke's Champagne' ♉ Popular, reliable, attractive early variety with deep red stems; 'Stockbridge Arrow' Deep red, heavy cropping, with thick, sturdy stems, ideal for early forcing and later outdoor crops; 'Timperley Early' ♉ Earliest cropping variety, slender, sharp, red and pale green stems, ideal for forcing

ASPECT Sunny, open site; tolerant of partial shade

SOIL Fertile, moist, well-drained soil; add well-rotted farmyard manure before planting; grow on raised mounds on heavy soil; pH6.0–6.8

PLANTING Plant 4–5-year-old crowns 2.5cm/1in below the surface, spacing 90cm/3ft apart and between rows, from November to December

CARE Keep weed free and remove yellowing leaves from neighbouring rhubarb plants to allow air circulation and space, so they don't swamp each other. Remove any flowering stems and mulch around the crowns in spring and again in autumn, taking care not to cover the crowns. Water regularly when growing, and do not allow the soil to dry out. For an early crop, force in winter by placing an upturned bucket or pot over the first shoots that appear, to exclude light. Stems should be ready to pick four to five weeks later and will be sweeter and more tender (and may not even need peeling)

PROBLEMS Slugs and snails

HARVESTING Don't harvest any crops in the first year to allow plants to establish; in year two, harvest about one third of the stems; in year three, pick all you like but always leave one or two stems on the plant. Pick stems young as they get tough and stringy the longer they are left. Pull stems rather than cut them when harvesting, by gently pulling the stalk from the base of the plant

YIELD 2.5kg/5lb per plant

GREENFINGER TIP *This is a crop that should do well for gardeners in cold areas as it thrives and flavours best in cooler conditions*

Strawberry
Fragaria × ananassa

EASY

'Gariguette'

'Royal Sovereign'

Strawberries are short-lived (cropping for three to five years), clump-forming perennials with fresh green, ribbed leaves, growing to 20cm/8in × 23cm/9in and spreading rapidly by runners. They bear a profusion of white or pink flowers in late spring and are grown for their very sweet, soft, red fruits. Strawberry varieties are categorised as early mid-summer, mid-summer and late mid-summer fruiters and can be grown in succession for (almost) continuous summer crops. Compact varieties are suitable for growing in containers or window boxes.

VARIETIES 'Cambridge Favourite' ♀ Vigorous, disease-resistant, with sweet medium-sized fruits; '**Elvira**' Large, firm, juicy, red fruits, some resistance to powdery mildew; '**Gariguette**' French variety with elongated, bright red fruits of outstanding sweetness, rare in UK shops; '**Royal Sovereign**' Almost as good as 'Gariguette', compact with excellent sweetness

ASPECT Full sun, with protection from frosts and wind

SOIL Fertile, moist, well-drained soil; add well-rotted manure or organic matter before planting; pH4.5–7.0

PLANTING Plant container-grown plants all year round as long as ground is not frozen or waterlogged, or buy bare-root, virus-free strawberry plants, sold as runners, and plant from March to April and July to September, depending on the variety. Space plants 30–45cm/12–18in apart and 75cm/30in between rows, spread the roots apart gently and firm soil back round plants; if planting in flat (rather than raised) beds, plant each one on a slightly raised mound, as strawberries like good drainage. Growing strawberries through a plastic sheet mulch has the advantages of pre-warming the soil and keeping weeds at bay; keep the plastic stretched taut to avoid puddles forming, which can lead to fruit rotting

CARE Mulch with garden compost to help retain moisture. Water regularly to help plants establish and, especially once the fruit begins to form, watering at the base of the plants; avoid wetting the leaves as this helps prevent *Botrytis* (grey mould). Remove the flowers in the first year on spring planted crops to help build the plant's vigour. Place straw under the plants once they show the first green fruits, to keep them off the soil; this prevents splashing and disease and also helps keep fruits clean. Slug and snail watch is a necessity. Protect fruit from birds with netting. Feed plants in containers or growbags with tomato feed from flowering to harvest. Remove any excess runners on a regular basis, cut back old leaves in autumn or early spring and replace plants every three to five years. To propagate, peg vigorous, healthy runners into the soil in spring; detach from the parent plant once rooted and before the parent flowers; expect fruit from these the following year

PROBLEMS Aphids, leatherjackets, slugs and snails; *Botrytis* (grey mould) and *Verticillium* wilt; birds

HARVESTING Pick individual fruits the year after planting, from July to September, once they have coloured up all over; pick berries for freezing when fruits still have a white tip. Pick on warm sunny days to preserve sweetness

YIELD 350–450g/12oz–1lb per plant

Walnut
Juglans regia

'Broadview'

Fallen fruit in autumn

Oh, how slow-growing is the old walnut tree! These trees get to about 10m/32ft in ideal conditions in ten years, but some varieties are only suitable for large gardens, reaching an eventual height and spread of 18–20m/60–65ft. Smaller varieties are available, but all are slow to mature, so you are going to need a lot of patience and space if you decide to grow walnuts. They are attractive large, spreading, deciduous trees with leathery, green, aromatic leaves, producing small greenish flowers and catkins and oval, smooth-skinned, green fruits that house the nuts. They are easy enough to look after, but walnut crops aren't reliable: the male catkins ripen before the female flowers, so can shed pollen and drop from the tree before the female flowers are ready to receive it. All the suggested varieties are self-fertile, so need no other walnut tree for pollination.

VARIETIES 'Broadview' Grafted, compact tree, cropping within four to five years, good frost and walnut leaf blight resistance (10m/32ft × 10m/32ft); 'Buccaneer' Grafted Dutch variety, producing rounded nuts, ideal pollinator for all varieties (17–18m/55–60ft); 'Number 16' Grafted, heavy cropping, round nut variety, cropping in four to five years (40m/131ft); 'Rita' Grafted, small, fast-growing, extremely hardy variety, cropping in four to five years (7–7.5m/22–25ft)

ASPECT Sunny, sheltered site; with protection from frost and wind

SOIL Fertile, moist, well-drained soil; pH6.5–7.0

PLANTING Try to buy a three- to four-year-old, partly trained tree or you won't see a crop for years. Plant both container-grown and bare-root trees from November to January (root development begins as early as February), at a minimum distance of 12m/40ft away from other garden plants as walnuts leak chemicals into the soil that prevent other plants growing well. Stake young trees

CARE Keep young trees well watered until they are established and mulch in spring. Pull suckers from grafted trees as they appear

PRUNING Prune minimally in subsequent years, removing dead, diseased, crowded, crossing and damaged stems in October (otherwise trees will bleed sap); seal wounds with beeswax

PROBLEMS Walnut blotch and walnut leaf blight; birds (especially woodpeckers) and squirrels

HARVESTING Pick nuts for pickling in July, when shells are still soft; gather for eating in October, as the hulls start to crack, or let them fall to the ground. Clean off the shells, wearing gloves as the sap stains easily, and store in a cool airy spot to let them dry

YIELD Variable

WALNUT BLOTCH is a fungal infection that affects walnut trees. Leaves develop brown blotchy patches and fall prematurely. Blotching can also spread to the fruits. **WALNUT LEAF BLIGHT** is another fungal infection, causing angular black patches that appear first on the leaves (leading to premature leaf fall) and spreading to the fruits. In both cases, collect all affected fallen leaves and burn. No chemicals available.

Wineberry, Japanese
Rubus phoenicolasius

EASY

Wineberry is a bramble-like hardy biennial (canes grow one year and bear fruit the next). This deciduous climbing shrub is related to blackberries and raspberries, and has a height of about 2m/6ft and spread of 3m/10ft. It has bright green leaves with white felty undersides and produces small, white-flushed, pink flowers in early summer. The delicious, sweet fruits are orangey red and are almost entirely enclosed by the sepals. They dangle from bristly, crimson, arching stems, which look very attractive with late-winter sun glancing off them. Because the fruits are encased in tough calyces until they ripen, wineberry is less troubled by birds and insects than other soft fruits. It used to be quite hard to come by but far more growers offer it nowadays, and it is well worth the pursuit. It is just as easy to grow as raspberries, over a fence or against a wall, and is a rewardingly ornamental plant with delicious berries.

VARIETIES None

ASPECT Sun or partial shade, with protection from wind

SOIL Fertile, moist, well-drained soil; add organic matter or leafmould before planting; pH4.5–6.5

PLANTING Plant container-bought plants all year round as long as ground is not frozen or waterlogged, or plant bare-root plants from November to March, spacing plants at least 3m/10ft apart to allow for easy access for picking

CARE Tie in canes to wires stretched between cane supports. Mulch with garden compost in spring to prevent weed growth and retain moisture to the roots, as they struggle in drought conditions, and water well, especially when the fruit starts to darken. Feed with a general fertiliser in late spring; don't overdo the nitrogen or you will get all leaves, no fruit. Self-seeds freely

PRUNING Cut canes that have fruited to just above ground level from February to March, and tie in the replacements as they grow in late spring and summer. Cut back very vigorous canes by 30cm/12in from the tips in February

PROBLEMS Birds and wasps

HARVESTING Harvest ripe fruits when berries darken between August and September

YIELD 8kg/17lb of fruit per bush

GREENFINGER TIP *Grow them up against a fence or along a post and wires to create garden divisions*

Artichoke, globe
Cynara scolymus

MEDIUM

'Green Globe'

	J	F	M	A	M	J	J	A	S	O	N	D
Plant			●	●								
Harvest					●	●			●			

This very tall (60cm–1.5m/2–5ft), thistle-like
perennial is a member of the cardoon family
(don't confuse globe artichokes with Jerusalem
artichokes: the plants and crops are quite
different). The globe artichoke is an architectural
plant, with large silver leaves and attractive
purple or green thistly flower heads, which
attract pollinating insects. It is grown for the
edible, fist-sized, closed flower buds (which
become inedible if left to open and flower); the
fleshy, diamond-shaped, scaly leaves and hearts
of the buds are delicious steamed and served with
melted butter or vinaigrette. Plants do need
space: one will fill a 90cm/3ft square.

VARIETIES 'Green Globe' Compact, tightly packed,
green flower heads, good flavour (90cm–1.5m/3–5ft);
'Purple Globe Romanesco' Rounded, tight green
flower heads flushed purple, excellent, nutty flavour
(60cm/2ft × 90cm/3ft)

CROP ROTATION Permanent

ASPECT Sunny site, sheltered from winds and frost

SOIL Fertile, rich, well-drained soil; add leafmould or
organic matter to light soils; pH6.5–7.0 (life expectancy
is short when planted in heavy, wet soil in cold winters)

SOWING Unreliable from seed, so usually planted as
rooted offsets

PLANTING Plant offsets from March to April,
planting 5cm/2in deep, spacing 90cm/3ft between
plants and rows

CARE Protect young plants with straw or bracken
and/or fleece in winter, particularly in cold areas, and
provide stakes. Keep weed free, mulch and water crops
well until established. Remove flower heads in the first
year to allow plants to establish; in the second year,
restrict to three stems per plant for cropping, to
encourage larger flower heads. Plants get less
productive by years three or four, so replace up to one
third of the crop with new plants or offsets annually to
keep a successive regular crop

PROBLEMS Aphids, slugs and snails

HARVESTING In May to June, cut off the topmost
heads first with a short length of stem attached, just
before the scaly leaves open. The head should feel firm
to the touch and the leaves soft and fleshy. Pick the
remainder in the same way, leaving the smaller heads
to ripen for a second, smaller crop in September

YIELD Up to a dozen flower heads per plant

Artichoke, Jerusalem
Helianthus tuberosus

Jerusalem artichoke plants

Jerusalem artichoke tubers

	J	F	M	A	M	J	J	A	S	O	N	D
Plant		●	●	●	●							
Harvest	●	●									●	●

This hardy perennial is grown for its edible, cream and pink, knobbly or smooth tubers, which are used as an alternative to potatoes (they can be boiled, roasted, stewed or baked and make fabulous chips). It is a very tall, vigorous plant that requires plenty of space as it can reach 3m/10ft × 60cm/2ft and is difficult to get rid of once established. It is related to the sunflower, and the tall stems have similar branched stems of shaggy, sunshine yellow flowers, which are very attractive to bees and butterflies. Because of their height, Jerusalem artichokes are very useful for dividing areas or creating shade. Portion control when eating them is advised as they cause dreadful flatulence!

VARIETIES 'Dwarf Sunray' White-skinned tubers requiring no peeling (2m/6ft × 60cm/2ft); **'Fuseau'** Smoother-skinned French variety with sweet, nutty flavour (3m/10ft × 60cm/2ft)

CROP ROTATION Permanent

ASPECT Sunny, open site; tolerant of partial shade

SOIL Fertile, moist, well-drained soil; add garden compost before planting or well-rotted farmyard manure; pH6.5–7.0

PLANTING Usually grown from tubers saved from the previous year's harvest. Plant from February to May, 10–15cm/4–6in deep, spacing 30cm/12in between tubers and rows

CARE Water well in the growing season and remove all flower buds to improve yields. Provide supports or earth up around the stems to 15cm/6in in May, when plants are 30cm/12in tall, to stabilise them. Cut stems down to 8cm/3in above ground level once leaves have yellowed, usually in September, or when frosts kill leafy top-growth. They are hardy and can be left in the ground all year, to be used as needed, but become invasive and deteriorate in quality if not lifted entirely; plant fresh tubers each year

PROBLEMS Slugs and snails; *Sclerotinia* rot

HARVESTING Tubers are ready for harvesting from November, once the foliage has died down. They are best lifted and used when needed, as they do not store particularly well

YIELD 15–20 tubers per plant

GREENFINGER TIP *If Jerusalem artichokes aren't lifted completely they quickly become an invasive weed, so it is worth installing a barrier around the roots when planting; many gardeners have a separate bed for artichokes, to limit their spread. If grown in the same bed every year, add extra organic matter at the end of each season to prevent the crop degrading*

Asparagus
Asparagus officinalis

'Connover's Colossal'

Asparagus officinalis

	J	F	M	A	M	J	J	A	S	O	N	D
Plant			●	●								
Harvest				●	●	●						

This hardy perennial has tall, slender stems with fine, ferny green foliage, and is grown for its delicious pale green stems, known as spears, that can be lightly steamed and served with melted butter, added to salads or eaten with vinaigrette. It requires a permanent site (a bed of 1.2m/4ft × 4m/13ft is about the minimum you will get away with) and can take up to three years to give a worthwhile bounty but can then crop for up to twenty years: you'll need both space and patience for this one.

VARIETIES 'Connover's Colossal' ♉ Early-cropping, thick-stemmed variety with heavy yields (90cm/3ft × 60cm/2ft); 'Crimson Pacific' Mid-season purple variety with sweet taste; 'Gijnlim' ♉ Early, green, thick-stemmed variety; good *Botrytis* resistance

CROP ROTATION Permanent

ASPECT Sunny, open site, with protection from cold winds

SOIL Fertile, deep, well-drained soil; on heavy soil, grow in raised beds; add well-rotted farmyard manure to base of trench before planting; pH6.6–7.5 (add lime if pH is below 6.0)

PLANTING Usually grown from one-year-old crowns. Plant fresh crowns without delay in March or April, in 25cm/10in deep trench lined with well-rotted manure, spacing plants 15cm/6in apart and 30cm/12in between rows; make 10cm/4in high mounds along the centre of the trench and site each crown on top, fanning the roots out evenly; gently backfill with earth, ensuring that each crown is about 10cm/4in below the soil surface so the buds are barely visible

CARE Keep beds weed free and water well in the first year. Earth up plants as they grow, leaving 10cm/4in of stem showing above the soil at each stage. Mulch with well-rotted farmyard manure as buds emerge, or topdress with a general fertiliser in spring and again once harvesting is over. Protect young spears with fleece in colder areas; do not cut back the foliage in the first two years, to give the crowns time to establish

PROBLEMS Asparagus beetle, slugs and snails

HARVESTING Do not harvest spears in the first year; harvest lightly in the second year, cut for six weeks only in mid-April to mid-June in the third year and cut for a full eight weeks in the fourth year. Harvest spears when they are about 15cm/6in high, cutting them 2.5–5cm/1–2in under the soil surface with a sharp knife

YIELD 20 spears per plant

ASPARAGUS BEETLE is a small black and red, yellow-spotted beetle; its grey larvae eat asparagus spears and leaves. Pick off by hand or spray with insecticide in the early evening.

Aubergine
Solanum melongena

'Black Beauty'

'Orlando'

	J	F	M	A	M	J	J	A	S	O	N	D
Sow			○	○								
Plant					●	●						
Harvest							●	●	●			

This tender perennial is normally grown as an annual in colder regions of the UK, and is a bushy, hairy-leaved plant with purple flowers, varying in height from 50cm/20in to 1.2m/4ft. It is grown for the large, glossy, egg-shaped edible fruits (rich in vitamins E and K), with skin colours varying from pale yellows to deep blue-black, widely eaten in the Mediterranean and gaining popularity in the UK. They need a long hot summer to crop well, so unless you can offer a very warm sheltered site, try them in a greenhouse, or in a growbag in mild areas.

VARIETIES 'Black Beauty' Early maturing variety with large black fruits (1.2m/4ft × 30cm/12in); **'Orlando'** Compact plant producing non-bitter 'mini' fruits, 5cm/2in long (50cm/20in × 30cm/12in); **'Rosa Bianca'** Italian Heirloom with non-bitter rounded fruits, 12cm/5in long, with cream skin flushed with rosy purple striping (75cm/30in × 30cm/12in); **'Tres Hative de Barbentane'** French variety with dark purple fruits (70cm/28in × 30cm/12in)

CROP ROTATION Other

ASPECT Very sunny, warm site, sheltered from winds and frost; grow under cover in colder areas

SOIL Fertile, moist, light, well-drained soil; add well-rotted farmyard manure to sandy soil; pH6.5

SOWING Sow seed thinly indoors from March to April at 21–30°C/70–86°F, covering lightly; prick out into single pots when seedlings are 5cm/2in tall and grow on at 16–18°C/60–64°F; harden off two weeks before transplanting

PLANTING Transplant outdoors when flowers appear, around May to June, once there is no frost risk, spacing plants 60–75cm/24–30in apart and 75–90cm/30–36in between rows. They can also be grown in pots or growbags in a sunny spot

CARE When plants are 25–35cm/10–14in high, pinch out tops to encourage bushy growth. Mature lower leaves can be removed to assist air circulation, which is critical to good development and allows light to the plants. Water well in the growing season, and feed at two-weekly intervals with a high potash feed (liquid comfrey or tomato feed) when fruits start to swell; thin to one fruit per stem for larger fruits or 6–9 fruits per stem for smaller ones, around July; may need staking due to the weight of the fruits

PROBLEMS Aphids and red spider mite (under glass); *Botrytis* (grey mould) and *Verticillum* wilt

HARVESTING Pick in July to September whilst the skin is still glossy: the duller the skin becomes the more bitter the flesh

YIELD Half a dozen fruits per plant

Bean, broad
Vicia faba

'Aquadulce Claudia'

'The Sutton'

	J	F	M	A	M	J	J	A	S	O	N	D
Sow		●	●							●	●	
Harvest						●	●	●				

Broad beans are a hardy crop, normally grown as an annual. The upright, vigorous, bushy plants with fragrant, sooty black and white flowers usually grow to about 90cm/3ft (or 45cm/18in for dwarf varieties) with a spread of 38cm/15in, and are grown for their edible young beans concealed in plump green pods, lined with the softest fleece. They are without a doubt my favourite bean – rich in protein and fibre – the only downside is that their season is not nearly long enough. Sow in October to November for a June crop (in mild areas with light soils only) and March for main crops from July to August.

VARIETIES 'Aquadulce Claudia' ⚥ Early cropping, long-podded with pale green beans; 'Green Windsor' Heirloom variety, large beans of excellent flavour; 'Stereo' Tall, upright variety with sweet, small, white, tender beans, pods can be cooked whole (1.2–1.5m/4–5ft); 'The Sutton' ⚥ Dwarf variety with good yields of short pods and tender beans (30cm/12in)

CROP ROTATION Legume group

ASPECT Sunny, open site, with protection from winds

SOIL Fertile, moist, light, well-drained soil; add organic matter to light soil; don't plant where a legume crop has grown in the previous two years; pH5.5–7.0

SOWING Sow seed outdoors from October to November under cover, or from March to April in drills, sowing singly 5cm/2in deep, spacing 23cm/9in apart and 45cm/18in between single rows, 60cm/2ft between double rows. Taller varieties need staking; planting in staggered double rows will help the plants support each other. Bean varieties cross pollinate, so use fresh named seed if you are worried about crossing

CARE Autumn-sown crops will benefit from cloches. Keep crops weed free, and water regularly in the growing season. Water with comfrey feed at two-weekly intervals when crop reaches 30cm/12in. Once the lower flowers have opened, pinch out 12cm/5in of the top shoots to deter blackfly

PROBLEMS Aphids; pea and bean weevil; chocolate spot

HARVESTING Pick beans from June to August, picking from the lower areas of the plant first to encourage further cropping. They are best harvested as baby vegetables; if left to mature the beans will be larger but tougher, and you may need to remove the outer skin

YIELD 3kg/7lb per 3m/10ft row

CHOCOLATE SPOT is a fungal disease that leads to brown spotting or powdery streaking on leaves. Sometimes plants may die, but crops are usually edible though the pods are discoloured. It is caused by damp, humid or crowded conditions: keep plants well spaced and weed regularly to prevent crowding and improve air circulation. Destroy affected plants after cropping.

GREENFINGER TIP *Opt for March sowing if you have wet, heavy soil, as winter losses can be high*

Bean, French
Phaseolus vulgaris

'Borlotto Lingua di Fuoco Nano'

'Neckargold'

	J	F	M	A	M	J	J	A	S	O	N	D
Sow				○	●	●	●					
Plant						●						
Harvest							●	●	●	●	●	●

French beans are half-hardy annuals. There are two types: dwarf (45cm/18in) or the taller, climbing varieties. They have medium-sized, broad, oval, mid-green leaves and come in a bewildering array of colours: from red and purple to green and yellow pods. They are grown either for their long, edible pods, which are boiled or steamed whole, or for the beans inside the pods; these can be harvested half-ripe, to give flageolet or cannellini beans, or left to ripen, then dried for haricot or kidney beans. They crop generously, store well and are relatively problem free – ideal for the new grower. They are also suitable for smaller spaces as they grow vertically and make good divisions between crops.

VARIETIES CLIMBING 'Borlotto Lingua di Fuoco Nano' Italian variety, marbled, creamy-red pods and white beans speckled red (fresh or dried beans); '**Blue Lake**' Ever popular, generous cropping with pencil-like pods and white beans (fresh or dried for haricots) (1.5m/5ft); '**Neckargold**' Stringless variety, generous crops of bright yellow pencil pods DWARF '**Purple Teepee**' Stringless, purple-skinned, long, curved beans, green when cooked; '**Tendergreen**' Almost stringless variety, rounded, long, plump green pods; '**Triomphe de Farcy**' Extremely thin, green pods with excellent taste

CROP ROTATION Legume group

ASPECT Sunny, sheltered site, with protection from winds

SOIL Fertile, moist, well-drained soil; add well-rotted farmyard manure on poor or light soils; don't plant where a legume crop has grown in the previous two years; dislikes heavy or acid soils; pH6.5–7.5

SOWING For an early start, sow indoors in April, at minimum temperatures of 12°C/54°F, one seed per pot, 5cm/2in deep, keep moist and harden off around May. Sow seed singly outdoors in situ in May to July, two seeds per hole (thin to the strongest plant when large enough to handle), spacing dwarf varieties 15–22cm/6–9in apart and climbing varieties 30cm/12in apart and 45cm/18in between single rows; sow under cloches in cold areas

PLANTING All are vulnerable to frosts and cannot be grown outside without protection until early summer. Transplant indoor-sown plants when 8cm/3in high, normally around June, spacing as above

CARE Provide supports for dwarf and climbing varieties. Water at the base, avoiding the leaves, and keep well watered, especially once flowering begins

PROBLEMS Aphids; slugs and snails; birds and mice

HARVESTING Pick beans young, when about 15cm/6in long and come away from the plant easily; pick often, to encourage new pods. Leave flageolet beans longer, to fatten. Leave beans for drying on plants until fully ripe and buff coloured, then hang indoors until pods dry and split open; dry beans on a sheet of paper and store

YIELD 4kg/9lb for bush varieties, 6kg/13lb for climbing per 3m/10ft row

Bean, runner
Phaseolus coccineus

EASY

'White Emergo'

	J	F	M	A	M	J	J	A	S	O	N	D
Sow				○	●	●	○					
Plant						●						
Harvest							●	●	●	●		

Runner beans are tender climbing perennials grown as annuals for their delicious, long, green pods and are amongst the best tasting of all the beans. They are tall (2m/6ft or more) plants with large, oval, mid-green leaves and red or white flowers and are heavy croppers (most people have a glut of beans to give away). They are ideal for screening areas in a vegetable garden, but do equally well growing up bamboo wigwams. Being tall they need protection from wind to stop them keeling over and are normally grown in double rows. Dwarf varieties (from 45cm/18in) are available for smaller spaces.

VARIETIES 'Scarlet Emperor' Generous cropping, long, slender beans with scarlet flowers; **'White Emergo'** ⚇ Weather tolerant variety with strong, long pods and white flowers

CROP ROTATION Legume group

ASPECT Sunny site, with shelter from wind

SOIL Fertile, deep, rich, moist, well-drained soil; don't plant where a legume crop has grown in the previous two years; pH6–6.8

SOWING For an early start, sow indoors in April, in a cool greenhouse at minimum temperatures of 12°C/54°F, one seed per pot (use deep pots or root trainers), 5cm/2in deep; harden off two weeks before transplanting. Sow outdoors in situ from late April, when all risk of frost has passed (use cloches to warm cold soil), one seed per hole, 5cm/2in deep, spacing 15cm/6in apart and 60cm/2ft apart for double rows; sow again in July for an autumn crop

PLANTING Runner beans are traditionally grown in trenches as they have deep roots; dig a trench 60–90cm/2–3ft wide, loosen the soil at the bottom and line with newspaper or well-rotted manure to help water retention in the root area. Insert single bamboo canes at least 2m/6ft tall along the rows or lash several together to make a frame for beans to climb. Transplant indoor-sown plants in June, spacing 60cm/2ft apart. Backfill trenches with well-rotted manure and fresh compost

CARE Keep well watered and do not allow to dry out once pods start forming, as this will result in a poor crop; water at the base of the plants, avoiding the leaves; mulch to help water retention. Encourage young shoots to climb up the canes; pinch out the growing tips (to encourage bean pods to form) when shoots reach the top of the canes

PROBLEMS Aphids; slugs and snails; mice and pigeons

HARVESTING Pick beans from July to October: the more you pick the more you will get. Pick when young or they become tough and stringy. If you leave them until the skins are rough and the bean is beginning to bulge through the pod, you've left it too late!

YIELD 6kg/13lb per 3m/10ft row

GREENFINGER TIP *Sow a few extra seeds at the end of each row as spares if any die or fail to come up*

Beetroot
Beta vulgaris

'Boltardy'

'Golden Detroit'

	J	F	M	A	M	J	J	A	S	O	N	D
Sow			○	◐	●	●	●					
Plant				●	●							
Harvest						●	●	●	●	●		

Beetroot is a quick and easy, low-maintenance crop, normally grown as an annual, that suffers from few maladies and is ideal for the new grower; it does well even in pots. It has ornamental green leaves with distinct red veining, similar to spinach, reaching a height and spread of 15–30cm/6–12in, and is grown for the round, edible, swollen root that develops at ground level, but you can use the young leaves too, in salads. The flesh is normally deep red to purple, but there are vivid varieties with cream, orange, yellow or even white flesh, and long or tapering shaped roots. Beetroot can be harvested until late autumn, and stored until March, but tastes best harvested when small and sweet. Beetroot is a notorious bolter: this can be caused by sowing seed early, so either sow bolt-resistant varieties indoors in spring or aim for the main sowing season outdoors (from May) to help prevent this.

VARIETIES 'Boltardy' ⚥ Round, firm, sweet-tasting, red variety with good bolt resistance; 'Forono' ⚥ Long, deep red, tapering variety with excellent flavour; 'Golden Detroit' Rounded, golden-skinned variety with good bolt resistance

CROP ROTATION Root vegetable group; catch crop

ASPECT Sunny, open site

SOIL Fertile, moist, light, well-drained soil; pH6.5–7.0 (lime acid soil)

SOWING Pre-soak seed in warm water for one hour before sowing. Sow seed indoors from March to April, two or three seeds per pot, 2.5cm/1in deep, thinning to sturdiest plant when 5cm/2in tall; harden off two weeks before transplanting. Sow seed outdoors in situ from late April to July, 2.5cm/1in deep, spacing single seeds 5cm/2in apart and 30cm/12in between rows, thinning when seedlings are 2.5cm/1in tall to 10cm/4in; sow at two-weekly intervals for a continuous supply

PLANTING Transplant indoor-sown seedlings into final positions when 10cm/4in tall, spacing as above

CARE Protect early sowings from frosts and young seedlings from birds with netting or fleece. Water regularly and generously in the growing season to prevent the roots becoming tough and woody, especially in dry periods

PROBLEMS Aphids; birds

HARVESTING Harvest spring-sown crops from June and summer-sown crops in September. Lift when young (the size of a pingpong ball for baby beets) for best flavour, or leave to increase for larger beets; harvest young leaves. For an early spring crop of new leaves, leave in the ground over winter, protected by a mulch. Store roots in boxes separated by sand in a cool, dark, dry place

YIELD 1kg/2lb of roots from a 3m/10ft row

GREENFINGER TIP *The generous foliage cover keeps weeding to a minimum*

Broccoli (Calabrese)
Brassica oleracea Italica Group

Broccoli plants growing in a netted coldframe

	J	F	M	A	M	J	J	A	S	O	N	D
Sow				○	○	○	○					
Harvest							●	●	●			

Calabrese (commonly known as broccoli) is a tall-growing (90cm/3ft × 45cm/18in) member of the brassica family, with large, ribbed, green leaves with crimped edges; it needs plenty of space. Calabrese is grown for its dense, green flower heads which are harvested before the flowers open, as the crop is inedible after this.

VARIETIES 'Fiesta' ⌧ Heat tolerant, very reliable variety producing dense, large green heads for late summer to autumn harvesting; **'Pacifica'** Deep green heads but not frost hardy; best for late summer to autumn harvesting; **'Tiara'** ⌧ Large, dense, green heads (350g/12oz) with excellent flavour

CROP ROTATION Brassica group

ASPECT Sunny, open site, sheltered from winds and frost

SOIL Fertile, moist, well-drained soil; grow after a legume crop or add organic matter before planting; don't plant where a brassica crop has grown in the previous two years; acid soil may need liming; pH6.5–7.5

SOWING Sow seed outdoors in situ from April to July, three seeds per station, 2cm/¾in deep and 30cm/12in apart, allowing 45cm/18in between rows; thin to the strongest plant when large enough to handle

CARE Keep weed free and water regularly. Plants may need staking or earthing up for support as the flower heads can become top heavy. Grow under mesh or fleece to deter cabbage butterflies

PROBLEMS Aphids, cabbage root fly, caterpillars and flea beetle; clubroot and downy mildew; pigeons

HARVESTING Pick when the central head is firm, with tightly packed buds; there should also be two or three heads on the side shoots

YIELD 225g/8oz of calabrese per plant (6 plants per 3m/10ft row)

'Fiesta'

Broccoli, sprouting

Brassica oleracea Italica Group

EASY

'Early Purple Sprouting Improved'

'Early White Sprouting White Eye'

	J	F	M	A	M	J	J	A	S	O	N	D
Sow			○	●	●							
Plant						●						
Harvest		●	●									

Sprouting broccoli is another tall-growing (90cm/3ft × 45cm/18in) member of the brassica family and is grown for its numerous, green, purple to white florets. It is similar to calabrese and enjoys much the same growing conditions, but is harvested in late winter or in the spring of the year after planting.

VARIETIES 'Early Purple Sprouting Improved' Early, reliable and generous cropping for spring use; **'Early White Sprouting White Eye'** One of the earliest varieties; tender, white uniform florets, reliable and prolific

CROP ROTATION Brassica group

ASPECT Sunny, open site, sheltered from winds and frost

SOIL Fertile, moist, well-drained soil; grow after a legume crop or add organic matter before planting; don't plant where a brassica crop has grown in the previous two years; acid soil may need liming; pH6.5–7.5

SOWING Sow seed thinly under cover in mid-March, in pots or modules, 2cm/¾in deep; thin to the strongest plant and harden off when plants are 8cm/3in tall. Sow outdoors from April to May into drills or a seedbed, 2cm/¾in deep, spacing 60cm/2ft between plants and rows, and protect from frosts

PLANTING Transplant, minimising root disturbance, when plants are about 10cm/4in high, in June, under cloches or after all frost risk has passed, spacing 60cm/2ft between plants and rows

CARE Keep weed free and water regularly. Plants may need staking or earthing up for support as the flower heads can become top heavy. Grow under mesh or fleece to deter cabbage butterflies

PROBLEMS Aphids, cabbage root fly, caterpillars and flea beetle; clubroot and downy mildew; pigeons

HARVESTING From February to March, snap off the flowering shoots when about 15cm/6in long, before the flowers open; pick regularly to encourage further shoots

YIELD 1.5kg/3–4lb per 3m/10ft row

GREENFINGER TIP *As with all brassicas, firm soil is the key to growing success*

Brussels sprouts
Brassica oleracea Gemmifera Group

'Peer Gynt'

'Rubine'

	J	F	M	A	M	J	J	A	S	O	N	D
Sow		○	●	●								
Plant				●	●	●	●					
Harvest	●	●						●	●	●	●	●

Brussels sprouts look just like miniature cabbages studded up thick green stalks, and are grown in much the same way as cabbages. They reach a height of 90cm/3ft and spread of 45cm/18in, but there are some choice dwarf varieties for smaller plot holders. Gorgeous purple varieties are available, so if you loathe sprouts, as many people do, perhaps a change of colour could lead to a change of heart? Or try them mashed with garlic butter and black pepper.

VARIETIES 'Nelson' ☷ Early cropping, sweet tasting; 'Noisette' Mid-season variety with sweet, nutty flavour; 'Peer Gynt' Popular dwarf variety with button-sized sprouts; 'Rubine' Small, firm, purple-red sprout with outstanding flavour

CROP ROTATION Brassica group

ASPECT Sunny, open site

SOIL Fertile, moist, well-drained soil; grow after a legume crop or add organic matter before planting; don't plant where a brassica crop has grown in the previous two years; acid soil may need liming to reduce the risk of clubroot; pH6.0–7.5

SOWING Sow seed under cover in February, two or three seeds per pot or module, 2cm/¾in deep; thin to the strongest plant when large enough to handle and harden off when 10–15cm/4–6in tall. Sow outdoors in a seedbed from March to April, 2cm/¾in deep, spacing 8cm/3in apart and 15cm/6in between rows; thin any weak seedlings; protect from frost with cloches

PLANTING Water plants thoroughly before transplanting and plant out from April to July, when 10–15cm/4–6in tall, spacing 60cm/2ft apart and between rows, and planting deeper than in the seedbed, with the lowest leaf just touching the soil; firm in well

CARE Keep weed free and water regularly. Earth up stems for extra stability or support plants with bamboo canes. Grow under netting to deter cabbage caterpillars and fit cabbage collars around seedlings to deter cabbage root fly. Mulch well in summer to help retain moisture

PROBLEMS Aphids, cabbage root fly, caterpillars and flea beetle; clubroot and downy mildew; pigeons

HARVESTING Frost definitely improves the taste of sprouts, so harvest after the first frosts for the best flavour, when they are about the size of a walnut, working your way from the bottom of the stems upwards. Once the stems are bare, pick the young leaves at the tops of the stems, known as sprout tops, and eat like spring greens. Alternatively, dig up the entire plant and hang it upside down in a frost-free place: the sprouts will keep for six weeks or so

YIELD 1kg/2lb per plant (5 plants per 3m/10ft row)

GREENFINGER TIP *Sprouts take up a fair bit of room, so save space by planting spring onions or radishes between the young plants*

Cabbage
Brassica oleracea Capitata Group

MEDIUM

'Pixie'

'Savoy Vertus'

Most of us are familiar with cabbages, with their edible, nutrient-rich leaves. They are very easy to grow (if you can keep the pests at bay) and, properly prepared and cooked, are undoubtedly delicious. The height and spread is about 30cm/12in, but there are many different varieties, from the upright, loose-leaved, pointed cabbages to the distinctive crinkled, green footballs of Savoy cabbage and the hard, smooth, bowling ball red cabbage, commonly used for pickling and mulling as a Christmas side dish. Quick-growing, crunchy Chinese cabbage can be harvested from September to November. Cabbages are normally grouped by their harvest times (spring, summer, autumn and winter). Spring cabbage attracts fewer pests than later-sown cabbages, so is ideal for the novice vegetable grower, and both spring and summer cabbages are useful for cut-and-come-again cropping. For cabbages year round, sow different varieties at different times; a small row sown every few weeks is more than ample for most growers' needs.

CROP ROTATION Brassica group

ASPECT Sunny, open site; tolerant of partial shade

SOIL Fertile, moist, well-drained soil; plant after a legume crop or add garden matter before planting; don't plant where a brassica crop has grown in the previous two years; acid soils may need liming; add bonemeal before planting out; pH6.5–8.0

SOWING Sow seed outdoors in pots or modules under cloches, or in a seedbed, sowing thinly 2cm/³⁄₄in deep; cover lightly with soil and water well until seedlings emerge; thin to strongest plant. For sowing times and spacings, see opposite

PLANTING Transplant once seedlings have at least four true leaves; water seedlings the day before moving from seedbed to final positions; make planting holes 15cm/6in deep, spacing as opposite, and label rows

CARE Water almost daily in dry weather then twice a week once established. Protect from root fly with cabbage collars and from pigeons with netting or mesh. Ensure newly transplanted seedlings do not dry out, by regular watering. Earth up stems of spring and winter cabbages to provide extra support, if needed, as they grow. Remove outer dead or damaged leaves

PROBLEMS Aphids, cabbage root fly, caterpillars and flea beetle; clubroot and downy mildew

HARVESTING For spring greens, cut young leaves from spring and early summer cabbages before the heart firms up; for hearted cabbage, wait until hearts are solid and cut off the heads or lift the entire plant; cut others as required, but lift red and white cabbages before the first frosts; winter cabbages can be left in the ground until needed as they are mostly frost hardy and slow to bolt

YIELD 750–1500g/³⁄₄–3lb per plant

SPRING

	J	F	M	A	M	J	J	A	S	O	N	D
Sow								●				
Plant									●	●		
Harvest				●	●							

VARIETIES 'Pixie' ⚥ Mid-green, firm, pointed, quickly maturing cabbage; ideal for early greens (collards) or harvest later as a small (hearted) cabbage; best sown in late summer for spring use; ideal in restricted spaces (20cm/8in × 30cm/12in); **'Wintergreen'** Hardy, heavy-cropping, loose-leaved variety, high vitamin (A and C) and mineral content

SOWING Sow seed outdoors, thinning to 15cm/6in between plants. Transplant seedlings to final positions, spacing 15cm/6in apart for spring greens and 25cm/10in for hearted cabbages, and 30cm/12in between rows

SUMMER/AUTUMN

	J	F	M	A	M	J	J	A	S	O	N	D
Sow			●	●	●	●						
Plant				●	●	●	●					
Harvest						●	●	●	●	●	●	●

VARIETIES 'Derby Day' ⚥ Balled, light green cabbage, good bolt resistance (30cm/12in × 30cm/12in); **'Greyhound'** ⚥ Pointed dwarf cabbage; good flavour (20cm/8in × 25cm/10in)

SOWING Sow seed outdoors, transplanting seedlings to final positions, 30–45cm/12–18in between rows and plants

WINTER

	J	F	M	A	M	J	J	A	S	O	N	D
Sow				●	●							
Plant					●	●						
Harvest	●	●	●							●	●	

VARIETIES 'Christmas Drumhead' Glossy-leaved, fast-growing, blue-green variety (30cm/12in × 45cm/18in); **'Savoy Vertus'** Frost-hardy, balled cabbage with crinkled deep green leaves; excellent flavour (30cm/12in × 45cm/18in)

SOWING Sow seed outdoors, transplanting seedlings to final positions, 60cm/2ft between rows and 45cm/18in between plants

RED

	J	F	M	A	M	J	J	A	S	O	N	D
Sow		●	●									
Plant				●	●							
Harvest									●		●	

VARIETIES 'Marner Lagerrot' Heavy cropping, deep red, balled, solid cabbage; excellent flavour; stores well (30cm/12in × 45cm/18in)

SOWING Sow seed outdoors, transplanting seedlings to final positions, 45cm/18in between rows and 23–38cm/9–15in between plants

CHINESE

	J	F	M	A	M	J	J	A	S	O	N	D
Sow							●	●				
Harvest									●	●	●	

VARIETIES 'Nikko' Crisp white ribs with long, dark green crinkly leaves ideal for stir fries; bolt resistant (28cm/11in × 13cm/5in)

SOWING Sow seed outdoors in situ, thinning seedlings to 30cm/12in between rows and plants. Water regularly in dry weather to prevent bolting. Ready to harvest 8–10 weeks from sowing

GREENFINGER TIP *To make your own cabbage collars, use 10cm/4in squares of carpet or underlay felt, slit to the centre and place on the soil around the stems*

'Marner Lagerrot'

VEGETABLES

Cardoon
Cynara cardunculus

EASY

'Gigante di Romagna'

Cardoon stalks

	J	F	M	A	M	J	J	A	S	O	N	D
Sow			○	○								
Plant					●	●						
Harvest								●	●	●		

This fabulously architectural, short-lived perennial is related to the globe artichoke and reaches a height of 2m/6ft or more. Both beautiful and delicious, it is grown in the herbaceous border as well as the allotment and has large, silver-white leaves with jagged, notched edges, up to 50cm/20in long, and purple thistle-like flowers. The leaf stalks are eaten, tied up to blanch the hearts just before harvesting and cooked like celery. It is a rarity in the supermarket (not surprisingly, as it looks like a whopping great stringy celery) but it has a delicate flavour, so why not give it a go?

VARIETIES 'Gigante di Romagna' Large-stemmed Italian variety with excellent flavour

CROP ROTATION Permanent

ASPECT Sunny, open site, sheltered from winds and frost

SOIL Fertile, moist, well-drained soil; add garden compost or organic matter before planting; pH6.5–7.0

SOWING Sow seed from March to April, under cover or in a heated propagator at a minimum temperature of 10–15°C/50–59°F, three seeds per pot, 2.5cm/1in deep; thin to the strongest plant when large enough to handle; harden off when plants are about 25cm/10in tall

PLANTING Plant out in May to June in trenches, 45cm/18in wide × 30cm/12in deep, lined with well-rotted manure; space 38cm/15in apart and 1.2m/4ft between rows, planting firmly, and backfill with soil

CARE Stake plants firmly. Water well and keep weed free. Mulch in spring with organic matter or garden compost. Blanch from August to September by gathering the central stems into a bunch, wrapping in corrugated cardboard, straw or newspapers and securing with garden twine; earth up the base of the plants to stop light getting in

PROBLEMS Aphids, slugs and snails

HARVESTING Four to eight weeks after blanching, unwrap one plant and check whether the stems are ready (they should be light green or very nearly white). Dig up the plant, cutting off the roots at the bottom and the leaves at the top, so what is left looks like a large bunch of celery, and use immediately

YIELD About 10 stems per plant

Carrot
Daucus carota

MEDIUM

'Chantenay'

'Resistafly'

	J	F	M	A	M	J	J	A	S	O	N	D
Sow	●	●	●	●	●	●	●			●		
Harvest						●	●	●	●	●	●	●

My first introduction to this orange taproot was courtesy of Peter Rabbit and although I can't bear cooked carrots, I absolutely adore them raw. They are biennials, but are usually grown as annuals for their swollen, tapered, orange-coloured roots, packed with vitamins A and C; they have attractive, fine, feathery, light green foliage reaching 30–38cm/12–15in. There are two main groups – early varieties sown in spring and maincrops sown in late spring to early summer – and different shapes and colours, from tapering purple, white or yellow varieties to small rounded roots that resemble turnips. They can be grown in containers or deep troughs in smaller spaces.

VARIETIES EARLY 'Chantenay' Fast-growing maincrop with short, stubby, deep orange roots; 'Mokum' Early, sweet, pencil-thin baby carrots, good in containers; 'Nantes 2' Medium length, quick growing, orange coreless, very sweet **MAINCROP** 'Autumn King 2' ☃ Maincrop and late-autumn carrot, with long tapered roots, stores well; 'Resistafly' Smooth-skinned, thick, mid-season or maincrop, good carrot fly resistance

CROP ROTATION Root vegetable group

ASPECT Sunny, open site

SOIL Fertile, moist, well-drained soil; add garden compost or leafmould to light soils; avoid stony, wet soils; pH6.5–7.5

SOWING Sow seed outdoors in situ, as carrots resent root disturbance, from January to July and again in October, sowing thinly 2.5cm/1in apart, 2cm/¾in deep, spacing 30cm/12in between rows; sow early spring crops when soil warms up to minimum temperatures of 7°C/45°F or pre-warm soil with cloches and protect from frost with cloches or fleece; thin to 10cm/4in between plants when large enough to handle (when thinning, pinch foliage sharply, as this minimises the smell of bruised foliage which attracts carrot fly). Early spring sowings give early summer crops, spring and early summer sowings give autumn crops and autumn and winter sowings (under cloches) give crops the following spring. Make successive sowings at fortnightly intervals for continuous crops

CARE Keep weed free and water well in hot dry weather. Do not add manure as it can make the roots split or fork. Grow under mesh or fleece or erect a barrier to deter carrot fly, or sow in early June to reduce threat

PROBLEMS Aphids and carrot fly; downy and powdery mildew

HARVESTING Dig up crops gently with a fork to prevent damage. Use at once or lift and store in a cool, dry place for winter use

YIELD 4kg/9lb from earlies, 5kg/11lb from maincrops from a 3m/10ft row

GREENFINGER TIP *Carrot fly cruise at low altitude, so build a barrier in the soil to 50–60cm/20–24in high, using wood, glass or a fine mesh; they will avoid the crop by changing direction rather than flying higher*

Cauliflower
Brassica oleracea Botrytis Group

Cauliflowers are grown for their large heads, often called curds, which are usually creamy white but there are also acid green, purple and orange-headed varieties available. They grow to 30–60cm/12–24in, and take up a lot of space, but mini varieties are available. Cauliflowers can be difficult for the novice as they are notorious bolters, need a lot of water, and winter varieties can be in the ground for some months. By choosing the right variety, it is possible to have cauliflowers right through the year, as there are winter, spring, summer and autumn varieties.

CROP ROTATION Brassica group

ASPECT Sunny, open site, sheltered from winds and frost

SOIL Fertile, moist, well-drained soil; grow after a legume crop or add organic matter before planting; don't plant where a brassica crop has grown in the previous two years; pH6.5–8.0

SOWING Sow seed thinly outdoors in a seedbed, 2cm/¾in deep, 15cm/6in between rows, with protection from frosts; thin to 8cm/3in apart when plants are large enough to handle. Follow the tables opposite for sowing times

PLANTING Transplant when seedlings are 2.5cm/1in tall, minimising root disturbance at all times. Water the seedbed the day before and plant firmly, planting up to the base of the first leaves so they develop a strong stalk, as they will be supporting heavy heads later. Space plantlets of spring, summer and autumn varieties 60cm/2ft apart, 45cm/18in between rows; winter 70cm/28in between plants and rows; mini varieties 15cm/6in between plants and rows

CARE Keep weed free and water regularly and often, or they run the risk of bolting and the heads will fail to develop. Tie up leaves in autumn to protect heads from frosts and keep them white (some varieties, such as 'Snowball', are self-blanching)

PROBLEMS Aphids, cabbage root fly, caterpillars and flea beetle; clubroot and downy mildew; bolting, boron deficiency and pigeons

HARVESTING Test that the heads are firm and tight and cut with a sharp knife; leave the leaves round the heads until you are ready to eat them

YIELD Five heads (or up to 20 for mini cauliflowers) per 3m/10ft row

GREENFINGER TIP *Don't dig the soil with a fork before planting – cauliflowers like firm ground*

'Grafitti'

'Snowball'

SPRING

	J	F	M	A	M	J	J	A	S	O	N	D
Sow			○									
Plant							●					
Harvest		●	●	●	●							

VARIETIES 'All Year Round' Very large creamy heads suitable for year-round sowing; freezes well; **'Purple Cape'** Hardy, with purple heads in spring

SUMMER

	J	F	M	A	M	J	J	A	S	O	N	D
Sow			○	○								
Plant					●							
Harvest							●	●				

VARIETIES 'Beauty' ☿ Smooth, large white heads, cropping August to September; **'Grafitti'** Dense purple heads, from summer to autumn; **'Idol'** Early sowing variety for crisp, white mini cauliflowers from June to July

AUTUMN

	J	F	M	A	M	J	J	A	S	O	N	D
Sow				○	○							
Plant						●	●					
Harvest									●	●	●	

VARIETIES 'Igloo' Plant closely for mini cauliflowers or space more widely for larger, dense creamy heads, from summer to autumn; **'Snowball'** Solid, white, compact heads for summer and autumn

WINTER

	J	F	M	A	M	J	J	A	S	O	N	D
Sow				○								
Plant							●					
Harvest	●	●	●									●

VARIETIES 'Autumn Giant' Popular variety with large, firm, white heads from November to December

Celeriac

Apium graveolens var. *rapaceum*

MEDIUM

Young celeriac

'Prinz'

	J	F	M	A	M	J	J	A	S	O	N	D
Sow			○	○								
Plant				●	●	●						
Harvest	●	●	●	●					●	●	●	●

Celeriac is related to celery, but grown for the swollen, creamy white, rough-skinned stem base. I think it quite an ornamental crop, with fresh green serrated foliage, growing to 60cm/2ft tall, and it's hardy to boot, but there is a fair amount of fiddling with side shoot removal to produce an underwhelming one balled root per plant, so you need the space to grow several plants. It has a subtle, celery(ish) taste – unbeatable braised but not to everyone's liking – and is probably only worth the effort if you adore celeriac. All varieties are much of a muchness; seed packets promise all singing and dancing non-bolting, pest and disease-resistant cultivars, but remain sceptical.

VARIETIES **'Marble Ball'** Commonly grown strong-flavoured variety, stores well; **'Prague Giant'** Rounded creamy bulbs, vigorous roots, stores well; **'Prinz'** Smooth, rounded bulbs, good bolt resistance; **'Snow White'** Good-sized creamy white bulbs

CROP ROTATION Root vegetable group; other

ASPECT Sunny, open site; tolerant of light shade

SOIL Fertile, moist, well-drained soil; apply bonemeal or organic matter before planting; pH6.5–7.5

SOWING Sow seed indoors from March to April in a greenhouse or heated propagator at minimum temperatures of 10°C/50°F, sowing thinly on the surface of compost; prick out emerging seedlings to one seedling per pot when large enough to handle, growing on at same minimum temperature; harden off in early May

PLANTING Transplant in late April to June, once risk of frosts has passed, spacing plants 30cm/12in apart and 45cm/18in between rows; plant so that the crown of the plant is just clear of the soil surface

CARE Water well, as roots tend to be small or hollow if allowed to dry out. As stems begin to swell, pull off the outer leaves and remove any side shoots as they appear, normally around July. The bulb tops will begin to stand proud of the soil as they develop. If leaving crops in the ground in winter, tuck up the plants with fleece or straw to protect from frosts

PROBLEMS Celery leaf miner, slugs and snails

HARVESTING Harvest from September or leave in the ground to use when needed; lift the entire plant with a fork, trimming off the roots and leaves

YIELD 225–400g/8–14oz per head

GREENFINGER TIP *Celeriac needs at least six months' growing time, from transplanting to harvest, for a worthwhile crop*

Celery
Apium graveolens var. dulce

TRICKY

'Daybreak'

Celery is grown for its crunchy leaf stalks, which are normally green, though pale red and yellow are available. The green leafy plants grow to 30–50cm/12–20in × 25–30cm/10–12in. Growing celery can be labour intensive; the traditional method involves regular earthing up to blanch stems and prevent them becoming stringy, though the result, known as trench celery, arguably has the best flavour. Self-blanching celery doesn't need earthing up but lacks the flavour and crispness of trench celery, and certainly won't put up with frosts. There are also leafy varieties, grown for the leaves rather than stems. For all celery, the soil preparation needs to be really good, the crop will not tolerate any hiccup in growth from water shortages and the pests it attracts can be tiresome. Choose the right varieties and you can have a crop for about half the year, but trench celery does require attentive supervision and skill, so sometimes the supermarket can seem a tempting option!

CROP ROTATION Other

ASPECT Sunny, open site; tolerant of partial shade

SOIL Fertile, moist, well-drained soil; apply well-rotted farmyard manure or bonemeal before planting; pH6.6–6.8

SOWING Seed can be difficult to germinate but celery seedlings are often available. Sow seed indoors from March to April in a heated greenhouse or heated propagator at minimum temperatures of 15°C/59°F; sow thinly on the surface in pots, trays or modules. Once seedlings emerge, keep minimum temperatures of 10°C/50°F to prevent bolting; prick out when large enough to handle and harden off when seedlings have four to six true leaves

PLANTING Plant out under cloches or when all frost risk has passed, at times shown in the tables overleaf

CARE Keep crops weed free and moist at all times, watering twice weekly, as the entire crop will become stringy and inedible if it dries out

PROBLEMS Celery leaf miner, slugs and snails; *Rhizoctonia* (plant rot) and violet root rot; bolting

HARVESTING To test celery for harvesting, snap off an inner stem: it is ready when it is tender and has no stringiness

YIELD 12 heads per 3m/10ft row (0.5kg/1lb each)

GREENFINGER TIP *Water, water, and water, particularly in dry conditions*

Celery (continued)

Celery growing

'Mammoth Pink'

TRENCH

	J	F	M	A	M	J	J	A	S	O	N	D
Sow			○	○								
Plant					●	●						
Harvest										●	●	

VARIETIES 'Mammoth Pink' Firm, crisp celery flushed pink stems; **'Solid White'** Sometimes sold as 'Giant White' (needs blanching), traditional tall, white-stemmed variety with excellent flavour

CULTIVATION Plant in trenches 40cm/16in wide and 30cm/12in deep, lined with added organic matter, 30–45cm/12–18in apart. Earth up plants by gradually filling the trench to soil level; if planted on flat ground without trenching, earth up soil progressively round the stems as they grow. Protect from frost with cloches

SELF-BLANCHING

	J	F	M	A	M	J	J	A	S	O	N	D
Sow			○	○								
Plant					●	●	●					
Harvest							●	●	●	●		

VARIETIES 'Daybreak' Long, smooth, pale green variety; good bolt resistance; ideal for summer cropping; **'Golden Self Blanching'** Reliable, fairly early (August harvest) yellow variety; average flavour

CULTIVATION Plant out in blocks rather than rows, spacing plants 25cm/10in apart. Pick from July to the first frosts; if left too long, the leaves turn yellow and the crop becomes stringy

LEAFY

	J	F	M	A	M	J	J	A	S	O	N	D
Sow			○	○								
Plant					●	●	●					
Harvest	●	●						●	●	●	●	●

VARIETY 'Kintsai' Dwarf, hardy, fast maturing

CULTIVATION Space plants and rows 30cm/12in apart. Pick and use leaves as needed

Chard, Swiss and Spinach beet

Beta vulgaris subsp. *cicla* var. *flavescens* (Swiss chard)

Beta vulgaris subsp. *cicla* var. *flavescens* (spinach beet)

'Bright Lights'

'Perpetual Spinach'

	J	F	M	A	M	J	J	A	S	O	N	D
Sow				○	○	○	○	○				
Harvest			●	●	●	●	●	●	●	●	●	●

Both Swiss chard and spinach beet are leafy beets, related to beetroot. Unlike beetroot, they are grown mainly for their leaves (the roots tend to be small and inedible). Both are pretty hardy and very easy for the novice to grow, suffering from few maladies or pests and offering a useful alternative to spinach. Swiss chard (also known as seakale beet) is the more ornamental, growing to 15–30cm/6–12in high, with deeply veined leaves in shades of yellow, ruby red and white. The leaves are used like spinach and the stems are braised like celery. Spinach beet (also known as perpetual spinach) has smaller leaves and is grown only for its leaves, which can be used young for salad leaves or as a spinach substitute.

VARIETIES SWISS CHARD 'Bright Lights' A new, tasty ornamental variety with orange, purple, white and red stems and vitamin-packed green leaves; young leaves can be used in salads or stir fries; 'Rhubarb Chard' ⚘ Very decorative and tasty with deep ruby-red stems and purple veins through dark green quilted leaves SPINACH BEET 'Perpetual Spinach' Large green leaves with very thin stems; great spinach alternative

CROP ROTATION Root vegetable group; cut-and-come-again

ASPECT Sunny, open site; tolerant of light shade; good for coastal conditions

SOIL Fertile, moist, well-drained soil; add well-rotted manure to light soils; pH6.5–7.5

SOWING Sow seed thinly outdoors in situ from April to August, 2.5cm/1in deep, allowing 45cm/18in between rows; thin to the strongest seedlings when large enough to handle, 10cm/4in apart for cut-and-come-again crops or 30cm/12in apart for larger-leaved plants

CARE Keep plants weed free, water regularly and mulch with grass clippings to trap moisture at the roots; protect with fleece in extremely cold conditions. Cut back the flowering shoots to keep the plant cropping. If the plant does not seem to be growing well, add a scattering of bonemeal, watering it in well, to help leaf development

PROBLEMS Slugs and snails

HARVESTING Leaves are usually ready to harvest between eight and ten weeks from sowing; late-summer sowings will mature through winter for harvesting in spring. Pick the outer leaves from both types gradually, not all at once; pick small young leaves for salads as needed or larger leaves from mature plants and new leaves will re-grow. Pick the stems when tender, about two months after sowing. Continue picking until the leaves get tough or the plant runs to seed

YIELD 6kg/13lb of leaves per 3m/10ft row

Chicory
Cichorium intybus

'Witloof Zoom'

'Rosso di Treviso'

Chicory is a perennial vegetable closely related to endive. There are three types: Belgian or witloof, grown for the chicons or crisp white leaf shoots, which need blanching; red radicchio, which forms slightly bitter, small, hearted plants a bit like Iceberg lettuces; and sugarloaf, which is like a looser-leaved, rounded lettuce. All chicory, whatever the type, makes excellent winter salad leaves. I think that the bitter flavour associated with chicory is much milder in home-grown crops.

CROP ROTATION Other; cut-and-come-again for radicchio or sugarloaf

ASPECT Sunny, open site; tolerant of light shade

SOIL Fertile, well-drained soil; tolerant of poor soil; pH5.5–7.5

SOWING Sow seed thinly outdoors in situ, 1cm/½in deep, with 30cm/12in between rows, thinning when large enough to handle to 23cm/9in for Belgian varieties and 30cm/12in for others

CARE Keep crops weed free and water regularly, though chicory is fairly drought tolerant

PROBLEMS Aphids, slugs and snails

BELGIAN

	J	F	M	A	M	J	J	A	S	O	N	D
Sow				●	●							
Harvest										●	●	

VARIETY 'Witloof Zoom' Tight, pale green chicons with white ribs

CULTIVATION Blanch, either by removing the leaves in September, leaving a stub of about 5cm/2in and earthing up with soil around the plant to 20cm/8in so that the chicons form under the soil, or cover with an upturned bucket; cut chicons just above the base of the plants, about one month after blanching, when they are about 15cm/6in high; the stump will re-grow with a second crop of smaller chicons; expect 3kg/6lb of chicons per 3m/10ft row

RADICCHIO and SUGARLOAF

	J	F	M	A	M	J	J	A	S	O	N	D
Sow				●	●	●	●	●				
Harvest								●	●	●	●	

VARIETIES RADICCHIO 'Rosso di Treviso' Tight, compact, white-ribbed, deep wine-red leaves, colours up best in cold weather SUGARLOAF 'Bianca di Milano' Upright chicory, looks a lot like cos lettuce, for harvesting autumn and winter

CULTIVATION Harvest from around August to the first frosts, when they are firm hearted and full headed, or leave and use when needed; leave stumps in the ground to re-sprout as a cut-and-come-again crop for a month or more; expect eight or nine heads per 3m/10ft row

Corn salad (Lamb's lettuce)
Valerianella locusta

EASY

'Cavallo'

	J	F	M	A	M	J	J	A	S	O	N	D
Sow				●	●	●	●	●	●			
Harvest	●	●	●	●	●	●	●	●	●	●	●	●

Everybody has gone salad mad and there are more salad leaves out there than I care to mention (and some, I swear, are largely decorative, cultivated by restaurants to make plates look pretty, but distinctly lacking in flavour). Lamb's lettuce is a fast-growing, hardy annual salad crop that reaches 15–20cm/6–8in in height and spread and is grown for its small, dark green, daisy-like leaves which have a delicate nutty flavour; there are also larger-leaved varieties. The flavour is strongest if used before spring. It's easy-peasy to grow as long as the slugs and snails are kept at bay.

VARIETIES 'Cavallo' Large-leaved variety with tangy flavour; good for winter cropping right up until first frosts; 'Louviers' Small, rounded, dark green rosettes of leaves with good frost resistance; 'Vit' Modern, vigorous, small-leaved variety, for cropping winter and summer

CROP ROTATION Other; cut-and-come-again; intercropping

ASPECT Sunny, open site; tolerant of light shade

SOIL Fertile, moist, well-drained soil; tolerant of poor soil; pH6.0–7.0

SOWING Sow seed thinly outdoors from April to September, 1cm/½in deep, in rows or blocks, thinning plants when large enough to handle to 10–15cm/4–6in apart and 15–20cm/6–8in between rows. Sow successively for continuous crops; sow in spring for a summer crop and in late summer for a winter crop

CARE Keep crops weed free and water regularly, picking off flower heads to prevent bolting (but leave flowers if you want plants to self-seed, which they do easily); protect autumn and winter crops with cloches

PROBLEMS Slugs and snails; bolting

HARVESTING Pick young leaves as needed in summer and winter (mature leaves become tougher with age); the more you pick the more leaves will grow and prevent bolting; or harvest the whole plant by cutting it at the base

YIELD Up to 20 heads per 3m/10ft row

GREENFINGER TIP *This is an ideal crop for window boxes or containers*

Cress, American (Land cress)
Barbarea verna

	J	F	M	A	M	J	J	A	S	O	N	D
Sow				●	●	●	●	●				
Harvest	●	●	●				●	●	●	●	●	●

A spicy-leaved salad, this tough little plant (about 15–20cm/6–8in in height and spread) has small, shiny green leaves and a peppery flavour. It is fabulous for winter salads, an easy crop for the veggie grower and ideal for container growing as it can be harvested four weeks from sowing. As it is shade tolerant, it can be planted at the foot of taller crops, such as sweetcorn or runner beans, allowing really efficient use of limited space.

VARIETIES None

CROP ROTATION Other; cut-and-come-again; intercropping

ASPECT Shady, sheltered site

SOIL Fertile, moist, well-drained soil; pH6.0–7.0

SOWING Sow seed thinly outdoors in situ from April to August, 1cm/½in deep, in rows or blocks, thinning plants when large enough to handle to 15cm/6in apart and 20cm/8in between rows. Sow seed directly into pots or containers, as above. Sow at fortnightly intervals from April for continuous crops through the summer to March of the following year

CARE Keep crops weed free and water regularly, especially in dry conditions, or leaves become tough. Protect autumn and winter crops with cloches or fleece

PROBLEMS Aphids and flea beetle; slugs and snails

HARVESTING Leaves are usually ready to harvest from four weeks after sowing. Pick the best-looking leaves; the lower areas will sprout again. Young leaves are more tender; mature leaves are tougher but become spicier with age

YIELD Up to 20 heads per 3m/10ft row

GREENFINGER TIP *Plant up a couple of pots outside the kitchen door for easy winter salads or garnishes and use unwanted thinnings in salads*

Cucumber

Cucumis sativus

MEDIUM

'Crystal Lemon'

'Marketmore'

	J	F	M	A	M	J	J	A	S	O	N	D
Sow			○	○	◍	◍						
Plant					●	●	●					
Harvest							●	●	●	●		

Cucumbers are from the same family as marrows and melons and have a climbing, bushy or trailing habit, with attractive, deeply lobed leaves and yellow flowers. Climbers grow to 2m/6ft × 90cm/3ft and compact cultivars to 60cm/2ft. Traditionally, cucumbers were grown in greenhouses, but many new varieties grow well outdoors in mild areas (though none are frost hardy). Outdoor (or ridge) cucumbers have rough skins and tend to be shorter than the smooth-skinned greenhouse cucumbers; some are suitable for use as gherkins. All can be grown in containers and growbags as well as in open ground.

VARIETIES **'Crystal Lemon'** Quick-growing ridge variety, rounded, apple-sized, yellow cucumbers; **'Futura F1'** Fast-growing, long, slim, dark green; **'Marketmore'** ♁ Strong, deep green, knobbly, ridge type, good disease resistance (outdoor only); **'Parisian Pickling'** Deep green, knobbly, ideal as gherkins or full size (outdoor only)

CROP ROTATION Other

ASPECT Sunny, sheltered site, with protection from winds

SOIL Fertile, moist, well-drained soil; add well-rotted farmyard manure on poor or light soil; pH5.5–6.8

SOWING Sow indoors from March to April, at minimum temperature of 20°C/68°F or in a heated propagator, two seeds 1cm/½in deep on their edges in 8cm/3in pots; remove weaker seedling when large enough to handle; harden off about four weeks after sowing, or transplant to final growing space under cover. Sow outdoors once risk of frost has passed, in mid-May (under cloches) to June, sowing two or three seeds 2.5cm/1in deep on their sides, spacing 45cm/18in between plants and 60–75cm/24–30in between rows; thin to the strongest seedling

PLANTING Transplant indoor-sown seedlings in late May (under cloches) to July, to above spacing. Plant two plants per growbag

CARE (for indoor and outdoor crops) Water generously and never allow to dry out; mulch in early summer to trap moisture at roots. Provide support for climbing types and tie in shoots with twine. Feed every two weeks with a tomato fertiliser once the first fruits start to swell. Pinch out growing tips to encourage fruit once plants reach the top of the support, or, for ground-grown cultivars, when five or six leaves are formed. For indoor-grown crops, nip out the tip of each side shoot at two leaves beyond a female flower (which has a tiny cucumber behind the flower) and pinch out tips of flowerless side shoots when they are 60cm/2ft long

PROBLEMS Red spider mite, slugs and snails; cucumber mosaic virus, powdery mildew and rots

HARVESTING Pick young cucumbers regularly to encourage further cropping; do not leave to yellow

YIELD 10 to 15 per plant

Endive
Cichorium endivia

'Cornet de Bordeaux'

	J	F	M	A	M	J	J	A	S	O	N	D
Sow				○	○	●	●	●				
Plant						●	●					
Harvest							●	●	●	●	●	●

Endive is a leafy, chicory-like lettuce, 35–45cm/ 14–18in tall. Varieties have frilly (or frisee) leaves or broad green leaves (these are hardier than the frillies). It is notorious for the slight bitterness in flavour that, like chicory, leads to loving or loathing, and it benefits from blanching to reduce bitterness. By sowing at monthly intervals you can have endive for six months a year, so that's a big plus in its favour.

VARIETIES FRILLY 'Pancalieri' Small, compact, frizzy leaves with rose-coloured midribs, self-blanching; **'Wallonne'** ⚥ Italian variety with fresh green leaves and creamy yellow at the centre **BROAD LEAVED 'Cornet de Bordeaux'** Closed heads with dark green, curled leaves, good frost resistance; **'Grobo'** Broad-leaved, mid-green, self-blanching heads

CROP ROTATION Other; cut-and-come-again

ASPECT Sunny, sheltered site; tolerant of light shade

SOIL Fertile, well-drained soil; pH5.5–7.5

SOWING Sow seed indoors from April, in a cool greenhouse at minimum temperatures of 20°C/68°F, sowing thinly in modules at 1cm/½in; thin when large enough to handle and harden off in May or June. Sow outdoors in situ from June, sowing thinly 1cm/½in deep in drills, thinning plants when large enough to handle to 23cm/9in apart for small varieties and 38cm/15in for larger, with 30–35cm/12–14in between rows. Repeat sow at monthly intervals until August

PLANTING Transplant indoor-sown plants in June to July, spacing as above

CARE Keep crops weed free and water regularly, especially in dry conditions. Blanch when the heads are full sized, about twelve weeks after sowing: either gather the leaves up in a bunch and tie them with twine (ensure leaves are dry or they may rot); or cover with an upended bucket to exclude light for 10–20 days, or place an old dinner plate upside down over the centre of each plant. Protect later crops with cloches or fleece

PROBLEMS Aphids and flea beetle; slugs and snails

HARVESTING Pick leaves as needed or cut whole heads from the base; the stump left in the ground will sprout anew

YIELD Nine to 12 heads per 3m/10ft row

GREENFINGER TIP *Don't be tempted to plant too early in the year as cold weather – temperatures lower than 5°C/41°F – can cause crops to bolt*

Fennel, Florence (Sweet fennel)
Foeniculum vulgare var. azoricum

TRICKY

'Cantino'

	J	F	M	A	M	J	J	A	S	O	N	D
Sow			○	○			●	●				
Plant				●	●							
Harvest							●	●	●		●	

Florence fennel, not to be confused with herby fennel, is grown for the delicately aniseed-flavoured, edible bulbous bases of the leaf stems and has light feathery foliage, reaching a height of about 90cm/3ft. It is a lovely ornamental plant that looks as good as it tastes, but enjoys a short growing season. Seed catalogues will tell you it is easy to grow, but being Italian, it is rather temperamental, expecting and needing a good warm summer to mature. In colder climates it grows quickly and spurts into flower before the base has had time to swell into anything that is halfway edible. Because of this tendency to bolt, try to grow bolt-resistant varieties if possible.

VARIETIES 'Cantino' Rounded compact bulbs with good bolt resistance if sown early; **'Perfection'** Good bolt resistance with large bulbs of excellent flavour; **'Romanesco'** Large, rounded, tightly packed, crunchy bulbs good for summer sowing; **'Sirio'** Italian variety with large, white, fast-maturing bulbs, ideal for late spring sowing for autumn harvesting

CROP ROTATION Other

ASPECT Sunny, open site; tolerant of partial shade

SOIL Fertile, moist, well-drained soil, preferably slightly sandy; add garden compost or leafmould; pH5.5–7.5

SOWING For an early start, sow indoors in a cool greenhouse or cold frame from March to April, sowing three seeds in modules (to avoid root disturbance), at 2.5cm/1in deep, thinning to one strong plant when large enough to handle; harden off two weeks before transplanting. Sow outdoors in situ in July and August, three seeds per station, 2.5cm/1in deep, thinning when large enough to handle to 30cm/12in between plants and rows. Plant bolt-free cultivars if sowing indoors or outdoors before mid-summer

PLANTING Plant out indoor-sown plantlets when they have no more than four true leaves, avoiding root disturbance; protect early crops with fleece or cloches, or plant when all risk of frost has passed

CARE Keep weed free; do not allow plants to dry out or get cold, as this will set the plant bolting. Once bulbs are about the size of a golfball, earth halfway up the bulbs to retain the whiteness and flavour; this also stabilises the plants and prevents them rocking

PROBLEMS Slugs and snails; *Rhizoctonia* (plant rot); bolting

HARVESTING Timing is everything. Cut them from the base when the bulbs are a good size (normally three months after sowing), but before they start to send up a flower stem (bolting) and become too tough to eat. The stub left in the soil will sprout new leaves that can be used for salads and you may even get some further small bulbs

YIELD 2–2.5kg/4–5lb per 3m/10ft row

GREENFINGER TIP *Florence fennel is a good companion plant to deter whitefly*

Garlic
Allium sativum

Garlic growing in rows

Elephant garlic

	J	F	M	A	M	J	J	A	S	O	N	D
Plant	●	●	●							●	●	●
Harvest					●	●	●	●	●			

Garlic is a herb derived from the pungent underground bulbs of a hardy, chive-like plant, about 60cm/2ft tall. The bulbs are creamy white and are made up of cloves that have papery white skin, often tinged pink. There are two types of garlic: soft-necked garlic does better in colder conditions, has smaller cloves and tends to store better (this is the stuff found in most supermarkets); hard-necked varieties are said to have a stronger flavour and are much easier to peel. Garlic is used widely in Mediterranean cooking and is deliciously sweet when roasted whole. The best crops come from late-autumn planting, as garlic likes a bit of chilly weather to form strong roots and good-sized bulbs. This is a totally idiot-proof crop, requiring little attention and space (and can be grown in containers), so there is no reason not to have a go. Elephant garlic (*Allium ampeloprasum*) is technically a leek but is grown and used like garlic; it produces large (10cm/4in) white bulbs with enormous garlic-like cloves and is popular for its mild flavour.

VARIETIES SOFT-NECKED 'Printanor' Firm white cloves and superb flavour; **HARD-NECKED** 'Spanish Roja' Very strong flavoured, connoisseurs' American variety; **'Thermidrome'** French, ivory white cloves, reliable cropping variety of excellent flavour

CROP ROTATION Root vegetable group; other; catch crop

ASPECT Sunny, warm, open site

SOIL Fertile, moist, well-drained soil; add leafmould or garden compost on poor or light soils; pH6.0–7.5

PLANTING Buy virus-free cloves and rub off the papery skins, separate the cloves and plant singly outdoors or in containers in October to March, 2.5–10cm/1–4in deep, pushing cloves into firm soil, pointed tip upwards, with the base plate facing downward; space 18cm/7in between plants and 30cm/12in between rows. Plant in spring for an autumn crop and in autumn for a summer crop

CARE Keep soil weed free and moist, watering well in periods of dry weather

PROBLEMS Rust and white onion rot

HARVESTING Harvest once the leaves start to yellow, but before they die back. Lift the bulbs gently to avoid damage and place on a wire rack or wooden tray until they have dried. They are traditionally plaited and should be stored in a light, cool dry place for up to 10 months

YIELD 18 bulbs per 3m/10ft row

GREENFINGER TIP *If growing from your own cloves, use the large outer cloves for best results*

Kale, curly (Borecole)
Brassica oleracea Acephela Group

EASY

'Dwarf Green Curled'

	J	F	M	A	M	J	J	A	S	O	N	D
Sow				●	●	●	●					
Plant						●	●	●				
Harvest	●	●	●	●							●	●

Curly kale is a member of the cabbage family, with loose, rather intriguing, crinkly, dark green leaves (though no heart to speak of). There are many varieties, with purple, red, green or blackish leaves; the dwarf varieties are ideal for the smaller plot (the larger ones can grow to 90cm/3ft × 60cm/2ft). Packed full of vitamins and with an endearing moniker, curly kale deserves to be more popular. Left to mature, the leaves are bitter, but choose the right variety, harvest early and steam or stir-fry, and it's undeniably delicious and crunchy. Curly kale can put up with poorer soil conditions than cabbages, and is less likely to suffer from clubroot and other ailments that plague the brassica family, so you should see good results first time.

VARIETIES 'Dwarf Green Curled' Compact, dwarf, Scotch variety with very curly, unusually sweet, deep green leaves; tolerant of wet, windy sites (45–60cm/18–24in tall); **'Pentland Brig'** Popular variety with blue-green, curly leaves, produces side shoots rather like broccoli spears as well as edible leaves (60cm/2ft); **'Red Russian'** ✻ Grey green leaves, purple stems, sweet flavour (90cm/3ft)

CROP ROTATION Brassica group; cut-and-come-again

ASPECT Sunny site; tolerant of light shade

SOIL Fertile, moist, well-drained soil; grow after a legume crop or add organic matter before planting; don't plant where a brassica crop has grown in the previous two years; acid soil soils may need liming to reduce the risk of clubroot; pH6.5–7.5

SOWING Sow seed outdoors in seedbed from April to July, sowing thinly in drills, 2cm/¾in deep, spacing 45–60cm/18–24in between rows; thin when large enough to handle, to 8–10cm/3–4in apart for cut-and-come-again crops or 60cm/2ft apart for full-sized plants. Sow in spring for a summer crop, sow in summer for an autumn/winter crop

PLANTING Transplant plants from the seedbed to final positions from June to August, when they are 10–15cm/4–6in tall (about eight weeks after sowing). Water the rows the day before planting out. Plant firmly, with the lowest leaves just above the surface

CARE Water transplanted seedlings well until established, then water sparingly (except in very dry conditions) or plants will be too lush to survive winter temperatures. Apply a nitrogen feed if leaves start to yellow, but don't overdo it as this can result in soft leafy growth that will not be frost hardy. Protect from birds with netting, and stake taller varieties. Remove any flower shoots as they appear

PROBLEMS Aphids, cabbage root fly, caterpillars and flea beetle; clubroot and downy mildew; pigeons

HARVESTING Cut leaves as needed from November to April; pick young leaves continuously as a cut-and-come-again crop, to encourage new growth

YIELD 1kg/2lb per plant

Kohlrabi
Brassica oleracea Gongylodes Group

'Azur Star'

'Purple Vienna'

	J	F	M	A	M	J	J	A	S	O	N	D
Sow			○	●	●	●		●	●			
Plant				●	●							
Harvest					●	●	●	●	●	●	●	●

Kohlrabi grows fast and is very easy to grow, so it is an ideal crop to give the novice veggie grower a confidence boost. Plants are about 45cm/18in tall, with large, cabbagey leaves (which are edible if harvested young) but it is grown for its turnip-like, sweet bulbs. These are odd looking, like small space aliens with unruly aerial tentacles, and can be white or purple skinned (which tend to be hardier) whilst the flesh is white. It is usually grown as a summer crop, but hardier varieties can be left in the ground until December in mild areas. As it is quick growing it is not as affected as other brassicas by pests and diseases. Sow at two- to four-weekly intervals for a continuous crop for half the year.

VARIETIES 'Azur Star' Purple skinned, ideal for early spring sowing, good bolt resistance; **'Olivia'** ꕥ Crisp, pale green bulbs with good fungal and mildew resistance; **'Purple Vienna'** Excellent purple-skinned variety for winter harvest

CROP ROTATION Brassica group; catch crop

ASPECT Sunny, open site

SOIL Fertile, moist, well-drained soil, preferably slightly sandy; grow after a legume crop or add organic matter before planting; lime acid soils to prevent clubroot; don't plant where a brassica crop has grown in the previous two years; pH6.0–7.0

SOWING For an early start, sow seed under cover in March, sowing three or four seeds in modules or trays, 2cm/¾in deep; thin seedlings to one strong plant when they have four true leaves; harden off in April. Sow seed outdoors in situ from April to August, when temperatures are reliably above 10°C/50°F (or crops have a tendency to bolt), sowing three seeds per station, spacing 23cm/9in between stations and 30cm/12in between rows; thin to the strongest plant when large enough to handle

PLANTING Transplant indoor-sown seedlings from April to May, before they are 5cm/2in high or they may bolt, planting out under cloches or when all risk of frost has passed; space 23cm/9in between plants and 30cm/12in between rows

CARE Keep crops weed free and water regularly in the growing season; the texture becomes woody if allowed to dry out

PROBLEMS Aphids, cabbage root fly, caterpillars and flea beetle; clubroot and downy mildew; bolting and pigeons

HARVESTING Harvest when bulbs are between the size of a golf or tennis ball, depending on preference. Younger bulbs are sweeter and more tender, but those left in the ground will retain excellent flavour and firmness. In mild regions, leave crops in the ground but lift before the first frosts

YIELD 20 bulbs per 3m/10ft row

Leek
Allium porrum

EASY

Planting 'Musselburgh' in late summer

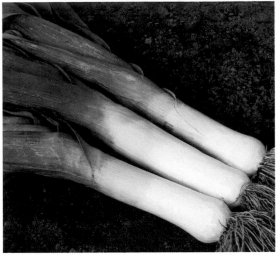

'Musselburgh'

	J	F	M	A	M	J	J	A	S	O	N	D
Sow	○	○	◑	◑								
Plant				●	●	●	●	●				
Harvest	●	●	●	●				●	●	●	●	●

Although leeks belong to the onion family, they hardly develop a bulb. Instead they are coveted for their long, smooth, straight white stems, which are green at the top and grow to about 38–75cm/15–30in tall. They are delicious chopped and sautéed in butter or added to soups and stews. Leeks can be sown for late-summer harvest, but they don't mind standing in the ground, bridging the winter harvest gap.

VARIETIES 'Musselburgh' Popular Scottish variety grown for its hardiness and reliable heavy cropping; **'Pandora'** Long, uniform, smooth white stems with dark green tops; some rust resistance

CROP ROTATION Root vegetable group; other

ASPECT Sunny, open site; tolerant of partial shade

SOIL Fertile, moist, well-drained soil; don't plant where onion crops have grown in the previous year; pH6.5–7.5

SOWING For an early start, sow under cover from January, sowing seed thinly 2.5cm/1in deep in pots or modules at minimum temperatures of 10°C/50°F; thin when large enough to handle; harden off about two weeks before transplanting. Sow outdoors in a seedbed from late March to April, sowing thinly 2.5cm/1in deep; thin when large enough to handle to about 5cm/2in apart

PLANTING Transplant indoor and outdoor-sown seedlings from April to August, when they are about 20cm/8in tall and pencil thickness, at a depth of 15cm/6in, spacing plants 15–20cm/6–8in apart and 30–38cm/12–15in between rows; make deep holes with a dibber, drop plant in (trimming the roots lightly with scissors if necessary) and puddle in with water to settle the roots. Don't backfill the hole: it will fill naturally over the coming weeks as soil is washed in

CARE Keep soil moist until transplanted seedlings are established, then water sparingly unless very dry conditions prevail. Apply a nitrogen feed in July to August or in February for late crops. Plant in deep holes or, if grown in flat ground, draw up soil around stems as they grow to exclude light

PROBLEMS Rusts

HARVESTING Lift from late summer (normally 4–5 months after sowing) or leave in the ground through the winter; dig up and heel in (dig a hole in a spare space and cover the roots with soil) if you need the space for another crop

YIELD 6kg/13lb per 3m/10ft row

GREENFINGER TIP *Try not to plant after potatoes in a crop rotation plan, as harvesting potatoes loosens the soil and leeks like the ground very firm*

Lettuce
Lactuca sativa

EASY

'Buttercrunch'

'Little Gem'

	J	F	M	A	M	J	J	A	S	O	N	D
Sow	○	○	◐	●	●	●	●	●	○	◐		
Plant			●	●	●							
Harvest			●	●	●	●	●	●	●	●	●	●

Lettuces are very popular salad crops, 8–15cm/ 3–6in tall, and there is a staggering choice of varieties available, with leaves that range from enticing fresh green to ruby coloured with frilly edges that look almost too pretty to eat. There are four main types: butterhead, cos, crisphead and looseleaf. The looseleaf lettuces just produce salad leaves, whilst others (such as cos) form hearts or heads. The butterheads tolerate poorer conditions than most other types and are generally summer-harvesting varieties. Crisphead lettuces are very popular and store well in the fridge. Lettuces grow rapidly and are best sown little and often, at fortnightly intervals, or else, like London buses, they all come at once. With the huge variety on offer it is possible to grow them nine months of the year, with winter protection (as they are not all hardy). Lettuces are excellent gap-fillers in a crop rotation and will do well in growbags, window boxes or containers.

VARIETIES BUTTERHEAD 'Buttercrunch' American variety with pale yellow, hard, compact hearts and crisp, light green leaves; **'Marvel of Four Seasons'** Red-leaved, solid-hearted variety with excellent flavour; can be sown all year but best harvested in spring and summer **COS 'Little Gem'** ♀ Quick-maturing, small, compact, cabbage-like heads with sweet flavour; **'Paris Island'** ♀ Large, upright variety with firm white hearts and pale green, crinkled, Savoy-like leaves **CRISPHEAD** 'Iceberg' Ever-popular variety, producing solid, round lettuces with crisp, crunchy, light green leaves; **'Webb's Wonderful'** The most widely grown lettuce in the UK (or so I am told); firm-hearted, crunchy, green, frilled-edge leaves; slow to bolt and tolerant of hot weather **LOOSELEAF 'Red Salad Bowl'** ♀ Looks much like endive, but with attractive, reddish, curling leaves, pick leaves little and often; **'Salad Bowl'** ♀ Like 'Red Salad Bowl', but with green leaves

CROP ROTATION Other; catch crop; cut-and-come-again, depending on variety

ASPECT Sunny, open site; summer varieties are tolerant of partial shade

SOIL Fertile, moist, well-drained soil; pH6.0–7.0

SOWING Sow early summer-harvesting varieties indoors from January, two seeds per module (to avoid root disturbance when transplanting); thin to the strongest seedling when large enough to handle and plant out under cloches in March. Sow all other varieties outdoors in succession at two-weekly intervals from March, sowing very thinly, using a pinch of seed, 1cm/½in deep in shallow drills; thin when large enough

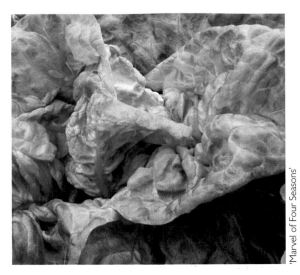

'Marvel of Four Seasons'

'Webb's Wonderful'

to handle to 25cm/10in apart and 30cm/12in between rows for butterhead varieties and 38cm/15in between plants and rows for cos and larger varieties

PLANTING Transplant indoor-grown plantlets from March to May, planting on a cool day, as hot sun can wilt, scorch or kill young plants. Lettuces don't transplant well, so plant out when they have six leaves, with the leaves just above soil level, avoiding disturbance to the roots

CARE Keep weed free and water well during the growing season, watering at the base of plants and avoiding the leaves. Lettuces have a tendency to bolt in dry weather; never let them go short of water, particularly in the two weeks before harvesting. Protect early-spring and autumn sowings with cloches

PROBLEMS Aphids, cutworm, leatherjackets, slugs and snails; *Botrytis* (grey mould), downy mildew and *Sclerotinia* rot; bolting

HARVESTING Lettuces take eight to fifteen weeks from sowing to harvest; but late summer and autumn sowings will be ready in spring. Pick firm-hearted lettuces as soon as they are ready or they will bolt. Cut looseleaf varieties whole or use for baby salad leaves by picking the outer leaves; new ones will grow to replace them

YIELD Eight or more heads per 3m/10ft row

Slugs and snails . . .

City-dwelling lettuce growers often bemoan the eternal struggle with snails and slugs getting to their lettuces first! I put this down to their being surrounded by brick walls, both large and small, where legions of snails can hide in damp, dark spaces until the lights go out. Trust me, before your head has even hit the pillow and long before you are punching out the Zzzz, those snails will be voraciously eating your crisp, fresh lettuce leaves, leaving nothing but slimed, ragged stumps by morning. My advice – lure the pests to a slug pub or visit the local farmers' market.

GREENFINGER TIP *Leafy lettuces such as 'Salad Bowl' varieties can be grown as a cut-and-come-again crop*

Marrow, Courgette (Zucchini) and Summer squash

Cucurbita pepo (marrow)

'Badger Cross'

Cucurbita pepo (courgette)

EASY

'All Green Bush'

	J	F	M	A	M	J	J	A	S	O	N	D
Sow				○	○	○						
Plant					●	●						
Harvest							●	●	●	●		

Courgettes, marrows and summer squash come from the same family (which also includes pumpkins and winter squash) and are all grown in much the same way. They are very vigorous annuals with large leaves that grow as trailing or bushy plants, reaching about 30–90cm/12–36in in height, though the size varies widely. Trailing types tend to sprawl horizontally rather than vertically. Courgettes are grown for their small, firm, tender, seedless fleshy fruits and edible, gaudy yellow flowers, which can be fried in a light batter. They are actually baby marrows (and will grow rapidly to large marrows if left on the plant) but with superior flavour, and are quick and easy to grow. Marrows are long, striped, green torpedoes, whose main season is summer and autumn but most store well for winter use. Summer squash are grown for their swollen fruits, which come in various shapes, including rounded, flattened varieties (patty pan) that can be yellow to creamy white; none are hardy. They should be picked when young or they tend to be watery and pretty tasteless. Squash plants are commonly bushy, but there are trailing types available. In truth, I have yet to meet a marrow I liked eating, so I have had to rely on my fellow marrow lovers for their recommendations.

VARIETIES COURGETTE 'Albarello di Sarzana' Italian variety with pale green, speckled slender courgettes, resistant to powdery mildew; **'All Green Bush'** Compact variety with tender dark green skin **MARROW 'Badger Cross'** ☸ Heavy-cropping, compact, dark green marrows (15–20cm/6–8in) with distinct, creamy-green striping, cucumber mosaic virus resistant; **'Long Green Trailing'** Large, dark green marrows with pale striping **SUMMER SQUASH** 'Butternut' Pale-skinned with creamy, sweet orange flesh; **'Yellow Bird'** (patty pan) Bright yellow, flat, scallop-edged

CROP ROTATION Other

ASPECT Sunny, warm, sheltered site, with protection from winds

SOIL Fertile, moist, well-drained soil; add organic matter in autumn before planting; too much manure can result in all leaf, no fruit; pH5.5–6.8

SOWING For early crops or in cold regions, sow seeds indoors in a greenhouse from April to May unless all risk of frost has passed; harden off two weeks before transplanting. Sow seed outdoors in situ, in late May or early June, about 2.5cm/1in deep, with two or three seeds per station, under cloches, spacing 90cm/3ft between plants; thin to one strong plant when large enough to handle. (Place the seed sideways, so that the flat surface is not horizontal, to prevent rotting.)

PLANTING Plant out indoor-sown seedlings in situ in May or June, when all danger of frost has passed, planting 8–15cm/3–6in deep, spacing 90cm/3ft between plants and rows for bush types and 1.5m/5ft between plants and rows for trailing types

Cucurbita pepo (summer squash)

'Butternut'

Summer squash planted in raised beds

CARE Keep crops weed free (once established weeds will have a hard time competing against this crop). If they flower whilst still under cover they will need hand pollinating (see page 107). Water regularly and generously when flowering; mulch soil to preserve water to the roots. Apply a high-potash feed every 10–14 days once the fruit starts to swell; trailing types need less water and feeding than bushy types. For marrows only, apply a nitrogen feed such as tomato fertiliser. Protect from frost with cloches or fleece when necessary. Provide supports for trailing types and raise the developing marrows off the soil with an old brick or tile

PROBLEMS Slugs and snails; powdery mildew

HARVESTING Pick courgettes when they are young and tender (about the size of your finger) as they become tasteless the bigger they grow; regular picking encourages further cropping. Harvest marrows when about 20cm/8in long and store on a cool shelf with good air circulation; if you plan to store them, leave to grow as long as possible as the tougher the skin, the better they last once cut. Pick summer squash when they are 5–10cm/2–4in long, for the best flavour; they store well in a fridge for one to two weeks

YIELD 12 courgettes per plant, but the more you pick the more will grow – it is a notorious glut crop; four to eight small marrows or two large marrows per plant; six to eight small summer squash per plant

Companion plants: courgettes and nasturtiums

VEGETABLES

Mizuna and Mibuna

Brassica rapa var. *nipposinica* (mizuna) and *Brassica rapa* (mibuna)

EASY

Mizuna

	J	F	M	A	M	J	J	A	S	O	N	D
Sow				○	○	●	●	●	●			
Plant						●						
Harvest	●						●	●	●	●	●	●

These oriental brassicas, often called Japanese greens, are all the rage with restaurant chefs as salad leaves are so increasingly widely grown. Mizuna has rosettes of green foliage, similar to rocket, with serrated, feathery edges to the leaves, thin white stems and a distinct mustardy or peppery flavour. Slightly less trendy than mizuna, mibuna is very similar, with more rounded leaves and a milder flavour. Both reach about 23cm/9in and are easy, vigorous, almost idiot-proof growers. Mature plants can be harvested individually and they are very useful as cut-and-come-again crops for salads. They are normally bought as mizuna or mibuna seeds; named varieties don't seem to be sold.

VARIETIES None

CROP ROTATION Brassica group; catch crop; cut-and-come-again

ASPECT Sunny, open site; tolerant of partial shade in summer

SOIL Fertile, moist, well-drained soil; grow after a legume crop or add garden compost or leafmould to light soils; pH5.5–7.0

SOWING Sow seed thinly indoors in a cool greenhouse from April to May, sowing 1cm/½in deep, in trays or singly in modules; prick out seedlings from trays and pot up when large enough to handle; harden off two weeks before transplanting. Sow seed in situ outdoors in June and July, or under cloches in August and September, 1cm/½in deep, thinning to 10cm/4in apart when large enough to handle, allowing 23cm/9in between rows for cut-and-come-again crops or 45cm/18in for larger plants. Sow at three-weekly intervals for continuous crops

PLANTING Transplant indoor-sown seedlings to final positions in June, spacing as above

CARE Keep weed free and water regularly to ensure soil does not dry out

PROBLEMS Flea beetle, slugs and snails; clubroot; bolting in hot dry weather

HARVESTING Pick young leaves for salads as needed; new leaves will grow about six weeks later and each plant can be cut several times. For more mature plants, cut the whole plant just above ground level after six to eight weeks (the stumps left in the ground often re-grow)

YIELD Nine heads per 3m/10ft row

Mustard, Oriental
Brassica juncea

'Red Giant'

Harvesting salad leaves

	J F M A M J J A S O N D
Sow	
Harvest	

These mustard greens are generally sold as oriental or leafy mustard. The leaves, which may be crinkly or smooth or crimped-edged and coloured purple, green or red, have a real mustardy tang and contain more vitamins and minerals than almost any other vegetable. They can be harvested young for a mild taste or left on the plant to mature for a stronger flavour, and are delicious lightly boiled with chilli, ginger and garlic or used in salads or stir fries. They are quick to mature – only six to eight weeks from sowing – so are ideal as catch crops (or two weeks from sowing for cut-and-come-again use).

VARIETIES 'Green-in-the-Snow' Deep green, tooth-leaved mustard with white veining; young leaves ideal for stir fries; **'Red Giant'** Japanese mustard with large, crinkly, coppery leaves with white veining; good bolt resistance

CROP ROTATION Brassica group; catch crop; cut-and-come-again

ASPECT Sunny, open site

SOIL Fertile, moist, well-drained soil; grow after a legume crop or add organic matter before planting; pH6.5–7.0

SOWING Sow seed outdoors in situ from July to August, three seeds per hole, 1cm/½in deep, spacing 10–30cm/4–12in between plants and 25–45cm/10–18in between rows; thin to the strongest plant when large enough to handle

CARE Water seedlings and crops regularly, little and often rather than weekly soakings. Protect late-summer sowings with cloches

PROBLEMS Aphids, cabbage root fly, caterpillars and flea beetle; clubroot

HARVEST Pick leaves from September as required, normally about two months after sowing; the more you pick the more new leaves will grow

YIELD 1.5kg/2–3lb per sq m/sq yard

VEGETABLES

Onion, Shallot and Spring onion
Allium cepa Cepa Group (onion)

EASY

'Jetset'

'Red Baron'

	J	F	M	A	M	J	J	A	S	O	N	D
Sow			●	●								
Plant			●	●								
Harvest							●	●	●			

There is not a day goes by in our kitchen when we don't use an onion. They are usually grown as annuals for their hardy, edible bulbs. Maincrop onions (those with large bulbs) have skin colourings varying from golden browns to yellows, reds, browns, whites and purples. Growing from sets (immature bulbs), which are more disease resistant than seed, is the easiest route for novices, but growing from seed is also easy and cheap. Crops are usually sown or planted in spring to harvest in summer and autumn (although some people like to plant in autumn, when the ground is empty, for harvest in summer).

VARIETIES 'Ailsa Craig' Large, globe-shaped, popular onion with mild flavour (spring sowing); 'Jetset' ☃ Heavy-cropping, golden, smooth, rounded onion, slow to bolt; 'Red Baron' ☃ Red-skinned, medium bulbs with mild white flesh ringed purple; 'Sturon' Reliable-cropping, large golden bulbs with excellent bolt resistance (spring sowing)

CROP ROTATION Other

ASPECT Sunny, open site; tolerant of partial shade

SOIL Fertile, moist, well-drained soil; add organic matter to heavy and poor soils; don't grow where an onion crop has grown in the previous year; pH6.0–7.0

SOWING Sow seed outdoors under cloches in March to April, sowing thinly in drills, 1cm/½in deep, spacing seed 23cm/9in apart; thin seedlings twice, once to 5cm/2in apart and again, once seedlings are growing upright, to 10cm/4in apart. Dispose of surplus thinnings as these will attract onion fly

PLANTING Plant onion sets from mid-March to April, spacing 5cm/2in apart for smaller onions, 10cm/4in apart for larger onions and 23cm/9in between rows; make small dents in rows, push each bulb firmly into it (pointed end up) and draw the soil around them, leaving the tip showing

CARE Water well and keep weed free. If plants bolt (produce flowers), remove the flowers immediately

PROBLEMS Onion fly; downy mildew and onion white rot; bolting

HARVESTING Harvest from July to September, once the leaves have yellowed and died back. Lift from the soil gently and spread on wire or wooden slatted trays in the sun to ripen and dry, or place under cover if wet. Store onions in hanging bunches or trays in a light, cool, frost-free, dry place

YIELD 60 (small) or 30 (large) bulb onions per 3m/10ft row

GREENFINGER TIP *Plant onions next to a carrot crop as the scent can deter carrot fly*

Allium cepa Aggregatum Group (shallot)

'Red Sun'

Allium cepa (spring onion)

'North Holland Blood Red'

	J	F	M	A	M	J	J	A	S	O	N	D
Plant	●	●	●	●								●
Harvest							●	●				

Shallots are grown in clumps for their bulbous roots, which are smaller and milder in flavour than onions. They have long, narrow, straight, green aerial leaves, which are not edible. They are usually grown from sets, which are more disease resistant than bulbs saved from a previous year and are quicker and more reliable than seed.

VARIETIES 'Griselle' French variety with long, teardrop-shaped, browny-grey-skinned bulbs, said to have best flavour of all shallots; 'Red Sun' Heavy-cropping, large red-brown bulbs, mild flavour

CULTIVATION Plant bulbs (sets) into warm soil (use cloches on heavy, cold soils) in a shallow drill from December to April, pushing each bulb pointed end upward, level with the soil so just the tips show, spacing 15–20cm/6–8in apart and 30cm/12in between rows (plant 'Griselle' in October to December). Harvest from July to August, once the leaves have yellowed and died back, and lay them out to dry. Store stacked in boxes (with airholes) or plaited, as they do in France

YIELD Expect 180 bulbs per 3m/10ft row

	J	F	M	A	M	J	J	A	S	O	N	D
Sow			○	○	○	○	○	○				
Harvest			●	●			●	●	●	●	●	

Also known as salad onions or scallions, spring onions are a very quick-growing crop, harvested when young for the tender green stems (30–45cm/12–18in tall) and small, crisp, white or pinkish bulbs and eaten raw in salads (or in our house often added to mashed potato to make champ). They are essentially immature onions and can be sown in late summer for spring harvesting or in spring for summer crops. They are a good gap filler in summer as they don't need much room; they prefer light soils in a sunny spot, but can be planted wherever there is spare space.

VARIETIES 'North Holland Blood Red' Ruby red variety (autumn sowing); 'Ramrod' ♛ British variety with white, uniform bulbs (all year sowing)

CULTIVATION Sow outdoors, sowing a handful of seed 1–2cm/½–¾in deep in shallow drills, spacing 1cm/½in apart and 30cm/12in between rows. Sow at two-weekly intervals from March to June for a continuous crop through the summer; sow from July to August for spring harvest the following year. There is usually no need to thin. Harvest when plants are 15cm/6in tall (about two months from sowing). If left in the ground they will continue to grow so bulbs will be large and stronger tasting, which is a bonus

YIELD Expect 200-plus plants per 3m/10ft row

Parsnip
Pastinaca sativa

'Avonresister'

'Lancer'

	J	F	M	A	M	J	J	A	S	O	N	D
Sow				●	●							
Harvest	●	●	●	●				●	●	●	●	●

The sweetness of a honey-roasted parsnip is simply exquisite. The long, tapering, creamy or white swollen roots have a delicious flavour and are better for a touch of frost, which concentrates the sugars in the roots, adding to the sweetness. The fresh green leaves can be steamed or added to soups. The average plant is 30–38cm/12–15in tall and they are quite easy to grow, so are ideal for first timers.

VARIETIES 'Avonresister' Can be planted more closely than other varieties, so ideal for smaller plots, said to have best canker resistance; 'Javelin' ⚥ British, firm, smooth-skinned roots, some canker resistance; 'Lancer' Skinny, smooth-skinned, cream roots, ideal as mini parsnips; 'Tender and True' ⚥ Long, tapering, cream roots, some canker resistance

CROP ROTATION Root vegetable group

ASPECT Sunny, open site

SOIL Fertile, moist, well-drained soil; don't add any manure before planting; stony soil can cause misshapen crops; pH6.5–8.0

SOWING Sow seed outside in situ in April to May, 2cm/¾in deep in a furrow, either three seeds together, spacing 10–15cm/4–6in between stations for medium-sized roots, or 20cm/8in for larger ones, or thinly along the length of the furrow, allowing 30cm/12in between furrows. Keep well watered until germination (which can be slow). Thin when plants have about four leaves, to the spacings above

CARE Water regularly until established; then water sparingly and only in periods of drought so the ground doesn't dry out: sudden watering after an absence may cause the roots to split. Keep weed free, avoiding the roots when using a hoe as damaged roots can make crops vulnerable to canker. Feeding is not normally necessary, but apply a general fertiliser if growth is poor

PROBLEMS Carrot fly and celery leaf miner; downy mildew in dry weather, parsnip canker and violet root rot

HARVESTING Start harvesting about four months after sowing or when the leaves begin to die back, or leave them to catch the frost as this improves the sweetness enormously. Leave in the ground through the winter and lift for use as required, or lift, remove all the leaves and store in layers in boxes lined with sand or peat

YIELD 4kg/9lb per 3m/10ft row

PARSNIP CANKER Rough brown patches develop, sometimes triggered by carrot fly damage to the plant. Grow disease-resistant varieties where possible and avoid all damage during cultivation. Sowing crops later and spacing them closer can help reduce the risk.

Pea

Pisum sativum

EASY

'Sugar Snap'

	J	F	M	A	M	J	J	A	S	O	N	D
Sow		○	○	○	○	○	○					
Plant				○	○	○						
Harvest						●	●	●	●	●		

There is nothing more delightful than a fresh pea, and the very act of podding them, with a colander on your lap in a sunny deck chair, eases the mind. Peas are annual plants, climbing by use of tendrils, and have purple, white or pink flowers, depending on the variety. They are classed as early, second earlies and maincrop, with earlier varieties tending to be shorter (dwarf varieties are 45–60cm/18–24in tall) and bushy in habit, whilst later varieties are normally taller (up to 2m/6ft). The edible green seeds are usually eaten shelled from their pods, but mangetout (or snow) peas and sugarsnap peas are eaten whole, pods and all, when still young and tender. Their sweetness is down to natural sugars, which begin to decrease the moment they are picked, and that is why a home-grown pea tastes so much better than shop-bought produce. I was informed recently that one portion of garden-fresh peas contains more vitamin C than two large apples and more fibre than a slice of wholemeal bread; so all the more reason to grow your own.

VARIETIES EARLIES 'Avola' Short, heavy cropping, with bright green uniform pods; *fusarium* wilt resistant; 'Little Marvel' � Popular, heavy cropping, with shortish, paired, light green pods and small peas; can be used for petits pois SECOND EARLIES 'Jaguar' Tall, with dark green double pods; good mildew resistance; 'Kelvedon Wonder' � Compact, enduringly popular, early maturing and good yields (45cm/18in) MAINCROP 'Lincoln' Heavy cropping, dark green curved pods with sweet-flavoured peas; 'Pea Onward' Heavy cropping, with double, short, stubby pea pods PETITS POIS 'Waverex' Dwarf, heavy cropping, with uniform green pods and tiny, very sweet peas SUGARSNAP 'Sugar Bon' Dwarf early variety with smooth, tender, green, sweet-tasting pods; 'Sugar Snap' Tall variety with tender green peas; *fusarium* wilt resistant MANGETOUT 'Oregon' Tall, early variety with flat, broad, sweet-tasting pods; 'Sugar Pea Norli' French variety with small, smooth, deep green, sweet-tasting pods

CROP ROTATION Legume group

ASPECT Sunny, sheltered site, with protection from wind; summer crops are tolerant of partial shade

SOIL Fertile, moist, well-drained soil; add organic matter to heavy and poor soils; don't grow where legume crops have grown in the previous two years; pH6.0–6.8

SOWING Sow in succession (say, two varieties at monthly intervals) from March to July. For an early start, sow earlies outdoors in pots under cloches from February to March, sowing one seed per pot; harden off two weeks before transplanting. Sow all others

Pea (continued)

'Kelvedon Wonder'

Pepper, chilli and Pepper, sweet
Capsicum annuum (chilli pepper)

'Early Jalapeno'

outdoors in situ from March to July, protecting crops from frost with cloches. For single rows, make a shallow trench, 15cm/6in wide and 5cm/2in deep, flatten the bottom with a hoe, and sow seed singly, 5cm/2in deep, spacing 5–10cm/2–4in apart; space trenches 60–90cm/24–36in apart for short varieties or 1.5–2m/5–6ft apart for taller varieties. Backfill the trench, label and water well. Dwarf and tall plants both need supports, such as twiggy sticks or bamboo, chicken wire stretched between upright canes or posts, or pea netting

PLANT Transplant early sowings from March to May, when 10cm/4in tall and all risk of frost has passed, spacing as above

CARE Protect seedlings from mice with netting. Mulch the soil to conserve water at roots. Keep weed free and water well in dry weather after flowers start opening

PROBLEMS Caterpillars and pea and bean weevil; rots; mice and pigeons; slugs and snails

HARVESTING Harvest three to four months after sowing: harvest earlies from June to September (about twelve weeks after sowing); second earlies: June to October (fourteen weeks); maincrops: July to October (fifteen weeks). Pick when they are young and tender and therefore sweeter; picking every one or two days to encourage more pod production and prevent them growing too large

YIELD 3kg/6lb per 3m/10ft row

	J	F	M	A	M	J	J	A	S	O	N	D
Sow			○	○								
Plant					●	●						
Harvest								●	●	●	●	

Chillies come from the tropics, so they need both heat and humidity to grow well and are grown as annuals in this country. They have rounded, tapering leaves, varying from light to dark green and sometimes purple, with single white flowers, and reach about 38cm/15in. The seeded fruits vary in shape and colour and can be long and pointed or squat and rounded, with green skins that ripen to reds and oranges, and have a fiery flavour. Some varieties are hotter than others: Habaneros and Scotch Bonnet are super hot, Jalapenos medium and Hungarian Hot Wax slightly milder. Crops can be disappointing after a poor summer, but they are a fun crop to grow if you can offer a warm sheltered spot, in the ground, greenhouse or containers.

VARIETIES 'Early Jalapeno' Medium, shiny, smooth, deep green fruits ripening to red; medium hot; 'Habanero Orange' Small green fruits ripening to orange; very hot; 'Hungarian Hot Wax' ⅊ Smooth, glossy yellow fruits ripening to red; medium hot

CROP ROTATION Other

ASPECT Sunny, sheltered site, with protection from wind; outdoors under cloches, or in a cool greenhouse or polytunnel

'Hungarian Hot Wax'

Capsicum annuum (sweet pepper)   **TRICKY**

'Sweet Chocolate Pepper'

SOIL Fertile, moist, well-drained soil; best in light soil; improve heavy soils with garden compost or leafmould; pH6.0–6.5

SOWING Start early to improve the chances of ripened fruit. Seed needs a minimum daytime temperature of 18–21°C/65–70°F and consistent night temperatures of 16°C/60°F for effective germination. Sow seed thinly on the compost surface, covering lightly, in a heated propagator from March to April. Prick out when seedlings have leaves large enough to handle and grow on in 8cm/3in pots, at the same temperatures as above. Harden off two weeks before transplanting

PLANTING Transplant into warm ground in May or June, once all risk of frosts has passed, spacing chillies 40cm/16in apart and 60–75cm/24–30in between rows. Plant two plants per growbag or singly in containers

CARE Water regularly to avoid leaves or flowers dropping, and especially once fruits appear. Feed fortnightly with a general or tomato fertiliser when fruits start to appear

PROBLEMS Aphids, red spider mite and whitefly under cover; rots

HARVESTING Ripening will depend on weather. Pick little and often when they are green to encourage further crops, or wait for them to turn red, though yields will be smaller

YIELD 3–4kg/6–9lb per 3m/10ft row

GREENFINGER TIP *Hose down the interior of the greenhouse once or twice a week to ensure high humidity*

	J	F	M	A	M	J	J	A	S	O	N	D
Sow			○	○								
Plant					●	●						
Harvest							●	●	●	●		

Sweet peppers come from the same family as chilli peppers and are grown in the same way. They have large, oval, pointed, green leaves and simple, white, cupped flowers. The large, green, red or yellow sweet peppers (with hollow insides filled with seeds) hang from strong branching stems, which grow up to 90cm/3ft and need support. They are grown for their succulent flesh and are delicious roasted or can be eaten raw in salads. Like chillies, they can be tricky for the novice.

VARIETIES 'Bellboy' Compact plants, deep green, thick-skinned, firm peppers, ripening to red; **'Marconi Rossa'** Long, tapering, glossy, sweet green pepper ripening to red; **'Sweet Chocolate Pepper'** Thick-skinned, very sweet-tasting, green pepper, maturing to purple black

CULTIVATION As for chilli peppers, but space plants 45cm/18in apart and 60–75cm/24–30in between rows. Provide bamboo supports for the plants once fruiting. Cut from the plant with secateurs when green and they will produce more fruit, or wait to ripen to a good red colour, when they will have a sweeter flavour

YIELD About 4.5kg/10lb per 3m/10ft row

Potato
Solanum tuberosum

'Orla'

'Desirée'

	J	F	M	A	M	J	J	A	S	O	N	D
Plant			●	●	●							
Harvest							●	●	●	●	●	

Potatoes are a hardy perennial with purple-white flowers and large green leaves, growing to about 60cm/2ft tall. All parts that grow above ground are poisonous: fortunately, we only grow them for their edible swollen underground tubers. They are one of the most basic, widely used and commonly grown vegetables – used for chips, boiling, roasting and mashing. Potatoes are classed as first earlies (including new potatoes), second earlies, maincrop and late maincrop, according to their growing time. Salad potatoes and heritage varieties are also available. They are usually bought as seed potatoes or mini plants, and are easy to grow (they can even be grown in deep pots, stacked tyres or wooden barrels). There is such a wide range of varieties that it is possible to be harvesting them from summer to late autumn.

VARIETIES EARLIES 'Arran Pilot' Popular variety, reliable, high-yielding, kidney-shaped tubers; 'Orla' ☘ Pale-skinned, white-fleshed tubers, good resistance to blight, scab and blackleg **SECOND EARLIES** 'Ambo' Sometimes used as an early maincrop, dependable, with flushed red skins, reasonably high yields and a good all rounder for culinary use; 'Cosmos' Medium yields with large white tubers with waxy flesh ideal for baking, roasting and chips, good resistance to blight and scab, drought tolerant **MAINCROP** 'Desirée' Popular early maincrop, despite its vulnerability to scab. Potatoes are pale red with yellow flesh and much loved for roasting; 'Maris Piper' Favourite for generous early maincrops of large, oval, white-fleshed tubers, eel-worm-resistant, great for mash, baking and roasting **LATE MAINCROP** 'Cara' Pale golden potatoes, widely grown for the creamy white flesh, good storage qualities and blight resistance. Great for mash, baking and roasting; 'Sarpo Mira' Floury, red-skinned potatoes, good yields and blight resistance, suits wide variety of soil types; good storage qualities **SALAD** 'Anya' High-yielding variety of oval, waxy tubers with nutty flavour. Good resistance to scab, slight blight resistance; 'Charlotte' Popular French variety with great flavour and heavy yields of waxy yellow flesh; good storage qualities; 'Franceline' Waxy, red-skinned, oval, high-yielding salad potato with tasty yellow flesh **HERITAGE** 'Witch Hill' (second early) Worth seeking out for its exceptionally early cropping, good yields and outstanding flavour; smooth, rounded tubers, both large and small, golden skins and floury white flesh

'Cara'

'Anya'

CROP ROTATION Root vegetable group

ASPECT Sunny, open site

SOIL Fertile, moist, well-drained soil; add organic matter in autumn before planting; pH5.0–6.0

PLANTING Plant first and second earlies mid-March to April, spacing first earlies 30cm/12in between tubers, 60cm/2ft between rows, and second earlies 45cm/18in between tubers, 75cm/30in between rows; plant maincrops and late maincrops from April to May, spacing 60cm/2ft between tubers and 75cm/30in between rows. Make a shallow trench 15cm/6in deep, with small holes along the bottom, plant seed potatoes singly, chitted end up, cover with 5cm/2in of soil and label rows

CARE Keep crops weed free and water well in dry periods. Protect early crops from frosts if necessary. Avoid wetting the leaves of early and maincrops, to help prevent disease. Earth up when they are about 15cm/6in tall, gently drawing up the soil around the plants, leaving some 20cm/8in of foliage above the surface; repeat once or twice more in summer

PROBLEMS Cutworm, potato cyst eelworm, slugs, snails and wireworm; blackleg, potato blight, potato common scab and rots

HARVESTING Harvesting times vary according to the variety, but are roughly: first earlies: ten weeks from planting; second earlies: thirteen weeks; maincrops: fifteen weeks; late maincrops: twenty weeks. Lift just before they start to flower or scrape away the soil and have a quick look. Dig them out gently, let them dry for an hour or two, and store in an airy, cool, dark place in paper sacks. Maincrops can be left in the ground, but are vulnerable to pests and diseases, so dig them up before the end of autumn and store as above

YIELD 4.5kg/10lb (earlies) or 10kg/22lb (maincrop) per 3m/10ft row

Chitting

Seed potatoes need chitting about six weeks before planting. Buy certified seed potatoes in January (don't use supermarket potatoes). Stand in an eggbox or shallow tray with the rose end (the end with most eyes) upward and place in plenty of natural light. Shoots will sprout from the eyes; potatoes are ready for planting when these are 2.5cm/1in long.

Pumpkin and Winter squash

Curcubita maxima (pumpkin)

'Atlantic Giant'

Curcubita moschata, C. pepo (winter squash) **EASY**

'Blue Ballet'

	J	F	M	A	M	J	J	A	S	O	N	D
Sow				○	○	●						
Plant					●	●						
Harvest									●	●		

Pumpkins can grow to 4.5m/15ft in height and spread and the current world record is held by the Americans at 767kg/1,690lb! Pumpkins have tough orange skins and orange flesh, and make great lanterns for Hallowe'en. Winter squash come in a dazzling variety of shapes, sizes and colours and are increasingly popular, with great taste and texture. Both pumpkins and squash are delicious roasted or puréed and fabulous in soups and pies.

VARIETIES PUMPKIN 'Atlantic Giant' Large, segmented orange pumpkin; '**Tom Fox**' Superb, rounded, smooth ribbed, with orange flesh and good flavour (3–5kg/6–11lb) WINTER SQUASH '**Blue Ballet**' Unusual rounded fruits with blue-grey skin and deep orange flesh, good virus tolerance (1kg/2lb); '**Bon Bon**' Dark green, squat, boxy fruits with smooth orange flesh

CROP ROTATION Other

ASPECT Sunny, warm, sheltered site, with protection from winds

SOIL Fertile, moist, well-drained soil; add organic matter in autumn before planting; too much manure can result in all leaf no fruit; pH5.5–6.8

SOWING Sow seed indoors from April to May, in a heated propagator or heated greenhouse at minimum temperatures of 13°C/56°F, planting 2.5cm/1in deep, placing seeds sideways to prevent rotting, two or three per pot; thin to one strong seedling when large enough to handle; harden off two weeks before transplanting. Sow outdoors in situ in June, once all frost risk has passed, into soil warmed by cloches, sowing two or three seeds per hole, 2.5cm/1in deep; thin to one strong seedling when large enough to handle, spacing plants 90cm/3ft apart between bushy plants and 1.5m/5ft for trailing types

PLANTING Plant out indoor-sown seedlings from May to June, making a small raised mound with a depression in the top and planting in the centre, leaving a raised rim at the top to encourage water to the roots, help water drain away efficiently and prevent rot

CARE Keep crops weed free (once established weeds will have a hard time competing against this crop). If they flower whilst still under cover they will need hand pollinating (see page 107). Water regularly and generously when flowering; mulch soil to preserve water to the roots. Apply a nitrogen feed once the fruit starts to swell. Protect from frost with cloches or fleece when necessary. Provide supports and remove leaves shading the pumpkins

PROBLEMS Slugs and snails; powdery mildew

HARVESTING Harvest for immediate use or leave to grow as long as possible if you plan on storing them, as the tougher the skin, the better they will last once cut

YIELD One large or four or five small pumpkins per plant; one large or four to six smaller winter squash per plant

Radish
Raphanus sativus

EASY

'French Breakfast'

'China Rose'

SUMMER

	J	F	M	A	M	J	J	A	S	O	N	D
Sow			○	○	○	○	○	○	○			
Harvest				●	●	●						

WINTER

	J	F	M	A	M	J	J	A	S	O	N	D
Sow							○	○				
Harvest								●	●	●		

Radishes are grown for their small peppery roots and are used in salads; there is nothing tastier than a fresh radish dipped in salt. The variety is huge and the roots can be black, yellow, purple and white as well as the familiar red. There are winter radishes too, which are about the size and shape of turnips and take longer to mature (growing to about 45cm/18in tall). These are suitable for winter storage; they have a strong flavour and can be cooked in stews or used for pickling. Summer radishes are about 20cm/8in tall and can be grown in containers, troughs or window boxes for gardeners who are short of space. Winter types are hardy, but summer crops are not.

VARIETIES SUMMER 'French Breakfast 3' ☻
Elongated, crisp, mild tasting radish with rosy purple colouring flushed white at the base; 'Scarlet Globe' ☻ Rounded red radish with mild flavour WINTER 'Black Spanish Round' Black-skinned heirloom variety with

hot flavour and large globes of crunchy white flesh; 'China Rose' Long (12cm/5in) rose-pink roots with crisp white flesh; stores well

CROP ROTATION Brassica group; catch crop

ASPECT Sunny, open site; summer varieties tolerant of light shade

SOIL Fertile, moist, well-drained soil; grow after a legume crop or add organic matter before planting; don't plant where a brassica crop has grown in the previous two years; pH6.5–7.5

SOWING Sow seed of summer radishes in succession from March to September, sowing thinly outdoors in situ, about 1cm/½in deep; sow at two-weekly intervals for continuous crops, allowing 15cm/6in between rows; thin to 2.5cm/1in between plants when large enough to handle. Sow winter radishes outdoors in situ in July and August, 1cm/½in deep, spacing 30cm/12in between rows; thin to 23cm/9in between plants

CARE Keep weed free and water well, especially in dry conditions

PROBLEMS Flea beetle, slugs and snails; winter crops are vulnerable to cabbage root fly and clubroot

HARVESTING Summer radishes grow quickly and become woody and inedible if not harvested within a month or so from sowing. Winter radishes can take up to four months to mature; leave in the ground until autumn and lift in winter, as they can be damaged by frost. Pull them up like carrots and store in a cool, dry place ready for use

YIELD 2kg/4lb from summer varieties, 5kg/11lb from winter varieties per 3m/10ft row

Rocket (Arugula)
Eruca sativa

'Va-Va-Voom'

'Wild Rocket'

	J	F	M	A	M	J	J	A	S	O	N	D
Sow			●	●	●	●		●	●	●		
Harvest	●		●	●	●	●	●	●	●	●	●	●

This popular, peppery salad leaf from the cabbage family goes by various names, including roquette or rucola, and has dark green leaves with serrated edges on slender stems. The best I have ever tasted was picked from the wild in Turkey and served with just a squeeze of lemon over it, but it is easy to grow as a salad crop in this country. It can't bear heat but will take any fertile soil. The plants are small (8cm/3in), so it's a good crop for pots, growbags or windowsills. The flavour intensifies when leaves are left to mature; younger leaves have a milder taste.

VARIETIES 'Apollo' Fast growing with larger, rounded, tender leaves, excellent peppery taste but no bitterness, slow to bolt; 'Va-Va-Voom' (who thinks of these names anyway?!) Very quick growing, crops within three to four weeks, with pungent flavour of wild rocket; 'Wild Rocket' Very strong peppery flavour

CROP ROTATION Catch crop; cut-and-come-again

ASPECT Sheltered site, with partial shade

SOIL Fertile, moist, well-drained soil; pH6.0–7.0

SOWING Sow seed in succession from April, sowing thinly outdoors in situ or in outdoor pots or containers, 1cm/½in deep, in rows (allowing 15cm/6in between rows) or blocks, to suit your space. Sow again at two- or three-weekly intervals, when the earlier seedlings have two true leaves, and repeat this process through the summer. If sown thinly enough, no thinning is required; if sown too thickly, pull out weaker looking seedlings, spacing 15cm/6in between plants and rows, and use in salads. Protect seedlings sown in April or September from cold or frosts with cloches or fleece

CARE Pick leaves regularly and water well, especially in dry weather, to prevent bolting

PROBLEMS Flea beetle, slugs and snails

HARVESTING Plants are ready to harvest between four and twelve weeks from sowing. Pick young leaves for immediate use; either pick a few at a time, to encourage further growth, or cut the whole plant down to 4cm/1½in above soil level and it will sprout new leaves from the base

YIELD 10 generous bunches per 3m/10ft row

GREENFINGER TIP *For nervous novices, seed is available on seed tapes: the seeds are pre-spaced and stuck to tape, eliminating the guesswork!*

Salsify
Tragopogon porrifolius

EASY

Salsify flower

'Improved Mammoth Sandwich'

	J	F	M	A	M	J	J	A	S	O	N	D
Sow			●	●	●							
Harvest	●	●	●							●	●	●

Salsify is a hardy root vegetable that is easy to grow, and is becoming a firm favourite with restaurant chefs. It looks and tastes a bit like parsnip and, like parsnips, the roots sweeten with the effects of frost. It can be left over winter to harvest – the long, thin, green young shoots and flower buds (which are pink when open) taste more like asparagus, but will need blanching. There seems to be only one variety easily available, marketed under a variation of the same name ('Mammoth', 'Sandwich Island Mammoth' and other names), but another variety, 'Giant', is becoming more commonly available.

VARIETIES 'Giant' Long, thin, creamy coloured roots (up to 30cm/12in) with fragrant, mild parsnip flavour; 'Improved Mammoth Sandwich' Long, thin, pale, tapering mineral-rich roots

CROP ROTATION Root vegetable group

ASPECT Sunny, open site

SOIL Fertile, moist, well-drained soil, preferably slightly sandy; add garden compost or leafmould; pH6.8

SOWING Sow seed outdoors in situ from March to May, sowing thinly in drills, 1cm/½in deep, spacing 15–30cm/6–12in between rows and thinning to 10cm/4in between plants when large enough to handle; seedlings are not suitable for transplanting

CARE Keep crops weed free and water regularly in the growing season. If growing for the flower buds and young shoots, cover the leaves with bracken or straw in spring, when growth starts in earnest, to exclude light

PROBLEMS White blister

HARVESTING From October onwards, lift and use the creamy roots as required. Any roots left in the ground until the following spring will produce tender shoots which can be cut when about 12cm/5in long, and cooked like asparagus or used in salads; pick both unopened flower buds and shoots in spring. Roots will be productive for some years from the first planting

YIELD 1.5kg/3lb of roots per 3m/10ft row

GREENFINGER TIP *Drop the harvested roots into boiling water for five minutes before using and the skins will peel more easily*

Scorzonera
Scorzonera hispanica

EASY

'Russian Giant'

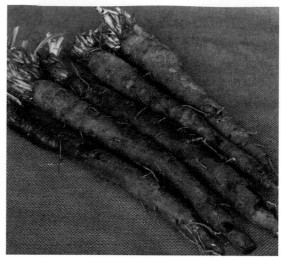

Scorzonera hispanica

	J	F	M	A	M	J	J	A	S	O	N	D
Sow			○	○	○		○					
Harvest	●	●	●							●	●	●

Scorzonera is another hardy root vegetable, widely grown in Europe, that looks like a spindly parsnip, with long, black, skinny taproots and firm, creamy white flesh. It reaches 60cm/2ft in height, with long, slender, spoon-shaped leaves at the top and bright yellow flowers in spring, and is grown in much the same way as salsify, though with a better flavour, in my opinion. The roots have a mild, sweet parsnip flavour. Young leaves and unopened flower buds can be eaten too, steamed or in salads. They last longer in the ground than salsify, and can be harvested right up to April. There seems to be only one variety widely available, which is a shame as veggies that are this easy to grow are always a pleasure.

VARIETIES 'Russian Giant' Long, black-skinned, tuberous roots with delicate flavour

CROP ROTATION Root vegetable group

ASPECT Sunny, open site

SOIL Fertile, moist, well-drained soil, preferably slightly sandy (stony soil can cause misshapen roots); add garden compost or leafmould; pH6.8

SOWING Sow seed outdoors in situ in March to May, and again in August for crops the following autumn, sowing thinly in drills, about 1cm/½in deep, spacing 15–30cm/6–12in between rows, and thinning to 10cm/4in between plants when large enough to handle. Seedlings are not suitable for transplanting

CARE Keep crops weed and pest free and water regularly in the growing season

PROBLEMS White blister

HARVESTING From October onwards, lift and use the roots as required. Any roots left in the ground until the following spring will produce tender shoots which can be cut when about 12cm/5in long, and cooked like asparagus. Pick unopened flower buds and leaves in spring, or cover with 15cm/6in of soil: new shoots will push their way through. Wash before boiling as they are prone to bleeding

YIELD 2kg/4lb of roots from a 3m/10ft row

GREENFINGER TIP *Scorzonera can be used as companion planting to carrots as it is said to repel carrot fly*

Seakale
Crambe maritima

MEDIUM

'Angers'

Seakale in flower

	J	F	M	A	M	J	J	A	S	O	N	D
Plant			●	●								
Harvest			●	●	●							

Seakale is a very hardy perennial that looks like a loose-leaved, grey-blue cabbage with white scented flowers. It can reach 90cm/3ft × 60cm/2ft but is grown for the delicious, asparagus-like young stems, which can be eaten raw but are usually lightly boiled or steamed and eaten with melted butter. The young outer leaves are also edible (taking a few from each plant along a row), as are the young flower buds and leaf midribs. It can be blanched to reduce any bitterness and to make the stems tender. It is a bit tricky to grow from seed and it can take two or three years before any edible stems are produced, so novices will find it easier to start off with root cuttings (thongs).

VARIETIES 'Angers' Drought-tolerant, hardy variety with crisp white shoots

CROP ROTATION Permanent; brassica group

ASPECT Sunny, open site

SOIL Fertile, moist, well-drained soil; grow after legume crop; add well-rotted farmyard manure or sand/grit to heavy soils; don't plant where a brassica crop has grown in the previous two years; pH7.0

PLANTING Plant thongs outdoors in final positions from March to April, spacing 38cm/15in between plants and rows

CARE Mulch with well-rotted farmyard manure in spring, or top-dress with low-nitrogen liquid feed or fertiliser. Remove flowering shoots to ensure stems grow well

PROBLEMS Flea beetle; clubroot

HARVESTING Grow for two years before cropping. Force plants in their second winter in November; stop cutting in May to allow plants to re-grow, for forcing again the following year, and grow on for a few years. For earlier cropping, bring plants indoors for forcing, and discard the whole plant afterwards. Harvest when stems are 10–20cm/4–8in long.

YIELD 8–10 stems per plant

Forcing

OUTDOORS Once crowns have died right back, around October until January, remove the rotting leaves and cover the crowns with about 8cm/3in of dry leaves or straw, then cover with a bucket or flower pot, blocking the drainage hole to exclude light. Stems will be ready for cutting within three months.

INDOORS After the first frosts, dig up the roots and leave them on the ground to expose them to frost. Trim off any side shoots, lay them in boxes in a cool place and exclude light by covering with black polythene. Stems are ready when they have turned white.

VEGETABLES

Spinach
Spinacia oleracea

'Giant Winter'

	J	F	M	A	M	J	J	A	S	O	N	D
Sow	○	○	○	○	○	○	○	○	○			
Harvest			●	●	●	●	●	●	●	●	●	

Spinach is a cool climate, hardy annual grown for its highly nutritious, deep green leaves that can be smooth or wrinkled. It is an upright, leafy plant growing to about 38cm/15in tall. Bolting (allowing the plant to flower) is the most common problem with spinach – it seems it can do it the moment your back is turned! There are varieties claiming to be bolt resistant, but even with these it is a bit of a gamble trying to prevent it. Planting them among taller crops that will offer shade is some safeguard against bolting, but you will get better at spotting the danger signs as your experience with the crop develops, so don't let it put you off growing it. Perpetual spinach (see page 55) is an easier alternative. Sowing different varieties in succession makes spinach available for nearly nine months of the year, including as young leaves for salads or stir fries.

VARIETIES 'Giant Winter' Large, crinkled, deep green leaves suitable for summer and autumn sowing, cropping in winter and spring; 'Matador' ⅋ Large, mid-green, lightly blistered leaves, for growing from spring to autumn; slow to bolt; 'Palco' ⅋ Large, dark green leaves, for early cropping as baby or salad leaves or as mature leaves

CROP ROTATION Root vegetable group; cut-and-come-again; catch crops (summer varieties only)

ASPECT Sunny, open site; tolerant of light summer shade

SOIL Fertile, moist, well-drained soil; add garden compost or leafmould to light soils; do not add manure to crop; pH6.5–7.5

SOWING For continuous crops, sow at two to three-weekly intervals from January to September; sow seed outdoors in situ in drills 2cm/¾in deep, spacing 2.5cm/1in apart and 30cm/12in between rows; thin seedlings when large enough to handle to 8–15cm/3–6in apart. For a continuous supply of cut-and-come-again crops, sow seed in mid-March to May in shallow drills, spacing 20cm/8in between drills, and cover lightly with soil; thin as above. Protect seedlings from pests. Seed does not germinate well in hot weather

CARE Keep weed free and water regularly, as crops that are left to dry out will inevitably bolt

PROBLEMS Downy mildew; bolting

HARVESTING Pick baby leaves when about 5cm/2in long from the outer leaves of each plant, or cut the whole plant 2.5cm/1in above the base, normally 10–12 weeks from sowing; new leaves will start growing from the stump

YIELD 6kg/13lb per 3m/10ft row

Swede

Brassica napus Napobrassica Group

TRICKY

'Best of All'

'Marian'

	J	F	M	A	M	J	J	A	S	O	N	D
Sow						○	○					
Harvest									●	●	●	●

Swedes are a hardy root vegetable, belonging to the brassica group, and are grown for their large rounded roots with pointed ends. The roots have tough, yellow to pink skins and are incredibly rich in vitamin B. Strong stems grow to 30–60cm/12–24in tall from the top of the swedes, with coarse green, oval leaves that make delicious spring greens if picked early in spring. The roots are sweeter and milder in taste than their relation the turnips. They aren't exactly a doddle to grow, and are in the ground for up to six months, but can be harvested from September onwards; if left in the ground for a short spell in winter they will sweeten with a touch of frost. For those of you who are partial to a swede (I disappoint you again, because I detest them – mind you, Bjorn Borg wasn't too bad!), here are a couple of worthy contenders.

VARIETIES 'Best of All' Reliable, sweet, white-fleshed, medium-sized swede; 'Invitation' Purple-skinned variety with good clubroot and mildew resistance; 'Marian' Clubroot and mildew resistant, reliable yellow-fleshed variety (the one to buy if you are a beginner); 'Ruby' Dark purple swedes with good flavour

CROP ROTATION Brassica group

ASPECT Sunny, open site

SOIL Fertile, moist, well-drained soil, preferably slightly sandy; grow after a legume crop or add organic matter before planting; don't grow where a brassica crop has grown in the previous two years; pH6.8

SOWING Sow seed thinly outdoors in situ from May to June, at 2cm/¾in deep, in drills, spacing 38cm/15in between rows, and thinning to 25cm/10in between plants when large enough to handle. Seedlings are not suitable for transplanting

CARE Keep weed free and water regularly in the growing season. Watch out for pests

PROBLEMS Aphids, cabbage root fly, caterpillars and flea beetle; clubroot, downy and powdery mildew

HARVESTING Lift from September to December, once roots are about 10–15cm/4–6in in diameter, or dig up earlier for mini veg. They can be left in the ground through the winter, but become woody with age, so are better lifted and stored for later use

YIELD 15kg/33lb from a 3m/10ft row

Sweetcorn
Zea mays

'Applause'

Sweetcorn growing

	J	F	M	A	M	J	J	A	S	O	N	D
Sow				○	●							
Plant						●						
Harvest								●	●	●		

Sweetcorn is a tall (2–2.5m/6–8ft), upright, ornamental cereal crop, with long, glossy leaves and tightly swaddled ears of corn. The sweetly succulent corn husks are usually bright gold, though there are some very ornamental red-eared varieties. It is rich in vitamins A and C, and you only have to take a bite of a warm, home-grown corncob coated in butter to know that it is a crop worth growing. It belongs to the grass family and is wind pollinated, which is why sweetcorn grows better planted in blocks, instead of rows. Crops can be disappointing if the weather is poor, as sweetcorn really needs long, hot summers to bring in a good crop. This is one crop that it pays to sow and plant on time.

VARIETIES 'Applause' So-called supersweet corn with large, firm, yellow cobs with high sugar levels; 'Minipop' Very sweet, crunchy baby corncobs; harvest the moment tassels brown; 'Sundance' ♣ Popular variety with large, sweet, creamy, yellow plump cobs, 18cm/7in long, grows better than most in poor summers

CROP ROTATION Other

ASPECT Sunny, warm, sheltered site, with protection from wind

SOIL Fertile, warm, well-drained soil; unsuitable for wet, heavy or very dry soil; pH5.5–7.0

SOWING Start early for the best chance of ripened corn later. Seed needs minimum temperatures of 20–27°C/68–80°F for effective germination. Sow seed indoors in April, in a heated propagator or heated greenhouse, at a depth of 2.5–4cm/1–1½in, in modules or root trainers (to avoid root disturbance later) then harden off and plant out when about 8cm/3in tall. Sow seed outdoors in mid-May into final planting positions, pre-warmed by cloches, 2.5–4cm/1–1½in deep, two to three seeds per station, spacing 35–45cm/14–18in apart and 45–60cm/18–24in between rows; thin to one strong plant when large enough to handle. Sow in blocks for the best crops

PLANTING Transplant indoor-sown seedlings when all danger of frost has passed (normally June), pre-warming cold soil with cloches and spacing as above

CARE Keep crops weed free but avoid damaging the roots when weeding, as they are very shallow. Protect the seedlings from mice with plastic bottles with both ends sawn off and protect the growing crop from birds and squirrels with netting. Start watering once the flowers appear and the cobs start swelling, or earlier under drought conditions. Earth up the stems to provide extra support

PROBLEMS Aphids; birds and mice

HARVESTING Test ripeness by pulling back the sheath and giving the heads a firm squeeze, or dig your thumbnail into the kernels: if they are ready to harvest they ooze a creamy liquid. Eat very fresh, as they lose their sweetness quickly

YIELD 10 cobs per 3m/10ft row

Tomato
Lycopersicon esculentum

'Beams Yellow Pear'

'Gardener's Delight'

	J	F	M	A	M	J	J	A	S	O	N	D
Sow		◐	◐	◐								
Plant						●	●					
Harvest							●	●	●	●		

Tomatoes are tender perennials, normally grown as annuals, and come from the tropics, so heat and humidity are vital for their development: they can't ever be exposed to frosts. The fruits are usually round and red, but can also be yellow or even brightly striped; the sizes and shapes vary from small cherry tomatoes through plump plum-shaped tomatoes to large beefsteak varieties. There are two main types: bush tomatoes are easier to grow, ripen more quickly and do better outdoors; vine tomatoes are slower to ripen and benefit from a warm greenhouse or polytunnel. There are dwarf varieties (30cm/12in) and taller varieties (60–90cm/24–36in). It is definitely easier to grow them than describe the process, and you can avoid the sowing process completely, if you wish, as tomato plants are widely available. I know people who have never grown so much as a weed before who have had great results with tomatoes first off. Plenty of sun and water are the keys to success. You can never have enough of a good thing and tomatoes certainly are just that.

VARIETIES 'Beams Yellow Pear' Yellow, small pear-shaped fruits with mild, sweet flavour (vine); 'Gardener's Delight' ☘ Widely grown, producing reliable generous crops of very sweet, marble-sized red tomatoes (bush); 'Marmande' ☘ Large, bulging, irregular, lightly seeded tomatoes, like the ones commonly seen in the Mediterarrean, but lacking the flavour they achieve there when grown in the UK (vine); 'San Marzano' Italian heirloom variety bearing red plum-shaped tomatoes; best for cooking; 'Tornado' ☘ Heavy-cropping bush variety, uniform, rounded, sweet red tomatoes

CROP ROTATION Other

ASPECT Sunny, warm, sheltered site or under cover in polytunnel or greenhouse; full sun

SOIL Fertile, moist, well-drained soil; add well-rotted farmyard manure or dress with a general fertiliser before planting; don't grow in the same place two years running; pH6.0–6.8

SOWING The sowing process is the same for indoor and outdoor tomatoes. Sow seed under cover in a heated propagator or at a minimum temperature of 16°C/60°F from February to April, sowing thinly and covering lightly with compost; maintain a steady temperature of 21–27°C/70–81°F once seedlings emerge and water regularly; prick out to larger pots when seedlings have three or four leaves, hardening off and planting out once all risk of frost has passed. Harden off plants that will remain indoors by opening greenhouse vents or polytunnel doors, for about two weeks, protecting from frosts. Plantlets are available, but they will need the above temperatures to grow well

Tomato (continued)

'Marmande'

'San Marzano'

PLANTING In May to June, when the roots are filling the pots or flowers begin to form, transplant to final growing positions outdoors (in open ground, growbags or containers), planting deeply and spacing 30–90cm/12–36in apart for bush tomatoes (depending on size) and 38–45cm/15–18in for vine types; allow 90cm/3ft between rows for all types. Pierce the bottom of growbags so water can drain away and plant two plants per bag or one plant per container. Provide support for all tomatoes, using bamboo canes, and loosely tie the main stem to the canes with garden twine

CARE Protect outdoor plants with fleece or cloches during a cold snap. Water regularly, never letting them dry out, but don't overwater, as this can diminish the flavour; little and often is best. Plants in containers and growbags need more watering as they dry out more quickly. Grow indoor plants in a cool greenhouse or polytunnel at the prevailing air temperature, with protection if cold. If growing under cloches or in polytunnels be mindful that they need insects to pollinate them, or they will not form fruit. Feeding regimes are the same for indoor and outdoor tomatoes: once the flowers have developed fruit, apply a liquid tomato feed or comfrey solution at two-weekly intervals. Remove yellowing leaves. Support with canes; tie stems in as they grow and remove any large stems that are overbalancing the plant. Pinch out side shoots and growing tips of vine tomatoes once four or five fruit trusses have formed, to encourage the plant's energy into fruit rather than leaf production: pinch out

the small side shoots that develop in the elbow where the leaves join the main and leaf stems

PROBLEMS Aphids, potato cyst eelworm and red spider mite; blossom end rot, *Fusarium* wilt and tomato blight; manganese deficiency

HARVESTING Pick when tomatoes redden (or colour up for the golden varieties) and eat fresh

YIELD Vine tomatoes up to 4kg/9lb per outdoor plant and up to 5kg/11lb per greenhouse plant; bush tomatoes 4kg/9lb per plant, depending on variety

....

GREENFINGER TIP *At the end of the season you will often be left with green tomatoes that haven't had time to ripen before the arrival of frosts. Ripen them indoors by placing them in a paper bag with a banana, which gives off ethylene gas. Green tomatoes are delicious fried or make great chutney*

Turnip
Brassica rapa Rapifera Group

EASY

'Snowball'

'Golden Ball'

	J	F	M	A	M	J	J	A	S	O	N	D
Sow			●	●	●	●		●	●			
Harvest				●	●	●	●	●	●	●	●	●

Turnips are quick-growing leafy plants, reaching a height of 30cm/12in, and usually grown as annuals. Their roots, which may be white, black or purple skinned, have a remarkably subtle sweet flavour; the leaves (turnip tops) are also edible. Maincrop varieties are hardier, take longer to mature and store better than the quicker growing early ones, whose roots are harvested young. If you choose varieties carefully you can have crops for eight months a year. I loathed turnips when I was younger, but in maturity I have discovered their joys, particularly when eaten young, as they should be. The young leaves (turnip tops) can be used as spring greens. Although a member of the brassica family, which is plagued by pests and diseases, they are pretty easy to grow.

VARIETIES EARLY 'Purple Top Man' One of the earliest cropping of the year with white skins flushed purple at the top; **'Snowball'** Very popular, quick-growing variety with white fleshed globes **MAINCROP 'Golden Ball'** Compact tidy plants with tender, yellow-fleshed roots; stores well; **'White Globe'** Rounded turnips with tender white flesh and skins, flushed purple at the tops

CROP ROTATION Brassica group

ASPECT Cool, open site; tolerant of light shade

SOIL Fertile, moist, well-drained soil; grow after a legume crop or add organic matter before planting; don't plant where a brassica crop has grown in the previous two years; pH6.5–7.5

SOWING Sow seed successively at three-weekly intervals, sowing early and maincrop crops from March. Sow seed thinly outdoors in situ, 2cm/¾in deep (pre-warm cold soil with cloches, cold frames or fleece), spacing 23–30cm/9–12in between rows. Thin seedlings to 10–15cm/4–6in apart when large enough to handle (but don't thin turnips you intend to use for their tops)

CARE Keep plants weed free and water regularly, especially in dry periods. No additional feeding is necessary if the soil has been well prepared

PROBLEMS Aphids, cabbage root fly, cutworm, flea beetle and wireworm; clubroot, downy and powdery mildew

HARVESTING Harvest turnips when they are about the size of a pingpong ball (about six weeks from sowing), or leave to develop if larger sizes are required. However, maincrop turnips will become woody if left in the ground too long, so dig them up in December and store indoors in boxes in a cool, dry place. Pick turnip tops when leaves are about 15cm/6in long (they will re-grow for another crop later) and cook as spring greens

YIELD 3.5kg/8lb from a 3m/10ft row of early varieties and 6kg/13lb for maincrops; about 500g/1lb of turnip tops from a 3m/10ft row

The plot

Finding space

As long as you have a windowsill, you can have fun growing small crops such as cress, radishes or sprouting salads. On a balcony or small patio with an open, sunny position, it is quite realistic to think of growing tomatoes, peppers, chillies, beans, herbs or a patio peach in containers or growbags. Even potatoes can be grown, in pots or stacked tyres, in a limited space. And some of these crops, such as climbing or runner beans, grow vertically on wigwams, which is a great space-saver. Admittedly, you are not going to be able to raise enough to keep the table groaning with home produce all year round, but you will certainly enjoy a moderate array of fare and the pleasure of eating your own fruit and vegetables.

A larger plot will allow the luxury of growing enough for your own needs, often with a surplus you can gift to friends, as well as broadening the range of fruit and vegetables grown. Some crops are only suitable for larger plots, as they demand large growing areas. These include cauliflowers, squashes and pumpkins. Others are perennials, and need a permanent site: they are grown in the same place year in, year out. These include asparagus, rhubarb, fruit bushes and trees. Think carefully before planting. For instance, fruit trees need an open, sunny position, but will eventually cast shade over any crops grown nearby, so site them with this in mind.

Consider growing fruit and vegetables in separate areas, where you can cater more easily to their differing needs. Growing fruit in fruit cages, which are walk-in, net-covered cubicles, will prevent the crops being looted by birds. Large spaces offer the luxury of an orchard, with the possibility of growing different and unusual fruit trees.

With more space you can accommodate a compost heap, a greenhouse and perhaps a potting shed in which to keep equipment. The possibilities are endless: the more adept you become at growing your own, the more ambitious your plans will become.

Allotments

The number of allotments has declined over the years, and the recent interest in growing your own means that demand now outstrips supply in some areas (yes, there is often a waiting list!). Apply to your local council, who manage allotments. The costs and sizes vary, but expect to pay £30–40 a year. Traditionally plots are about 250sq m/2,700sq ft but many councils will halve plots, and sharing a plot with family or friends is a great way to spread the labour and harvests. Check out the past history of your intended plot: it may have been tended organically, or neglected and left lying fallow. Don't be afraid to ask.

Choosing a suitable site

Soil is a critical factor in growing produce successfully but aspect is equally important, as almost all fruit and vegetables like an open, sunny position (exceptions to this include beans, endive, lettuce and spinach, which can all take some shade).

Fruit and vegetables need good light levels, protection from winds and fertile, well-drained soil. So a dank, waterlogged site that gets precious little sunlight is not going to prosper. If you have been able to grow a reasonable lawn on your proposed site, the chances are this area will be good enough to sustain a veggie plot.

As well as having fertile, well-drained soil, an ideal growing site will be:

- sunny, facing south or south-east
- in an open position, away from overhanging trees (which result in dry shade)
- in a sheltered position, free of frost pockets
- level (a sloping site can be prone to soil erosion)
- close to a plentiful water supply
- easily accessible for garden equipment, wheelbarrows and delivery of manures or other soil improvers
- weed free, or potentially weed free if you can reasonably clear it
- securely fenced, to discourage scavenging animals such as rabbits, foxes and deer

Designing the layout

Vegetable areas can be laid out in all sorts of patterns: cartwheels with a different crop in each segment, raised beds, square or rectangular beds, or in an assortment of containers on a patio. An increasingly popular option is the potager. This is a kitchen garden in which fruit and vegetables are grown alongside ornamental garden plants. This is an efficient and highly creative way of growing produce: the area manages to be both utilitarian and decorative.

A plot in open ground can be as large or small as you like, depending on personal preference and available space. The downside of an open plot is the danger of treading down and compacting the soil when maintaining the crops: weeding, hoeing, watering, sowing, thinning or harvesting.

A raised bed system is an alternative layout: a number of narrow, rectangular beds are enclosed by gravel boards, bricks or railway sleepers and the beds are divided up by paths. The advantages are that there is no need to tread on the soil whilst tending your crops, so they retain good soil structure and avoid

compaction; manures can be applied directly where it is needed, so there is less waste; and they minimise all that bending. Also, drainage is better and the soil tends to heat up quicker than in open ground. Although the bed system is more work initially, it is easier to maintain than wide open beds in the long run, and more space-efficient.

The length of each bed is entirely up to you; your choice of crops will certainly influence the size, but 3m/10ft × 1.2m/4ft is an ideal starting point. You can have one long bed, or three or four shorter beds, depending on the available space, but leave enough space between the beds to get your wheelbarrow up and down (about 90cm/3ft).

Clearing the site

To prepare a plot in open ground, first strip away any existing grass and eradicate weeds. If the weeds are tall, strim them down to ground level and compost all the top-growth. Then hand weed or dig out the remaining parts of the plants, roots and all. Make sure you remove all the roots,

---

MAKING A RAISED BED SYSTEM

Late autumn to winter is an ideal time to prepare new beds.

- Mark out beds with string, sand or spray marker, trying to ensure that each bed runs north to south, so that they all receive the same amount of sunlight.
- Dig over the existing soil, pull up any weeds, apply a thick layer of organic material to the surface and dig it in.
- Enclose the prepared soil with gravel boards, concrete blocks, railway sleepers or brick edging at a minimum height of 30cm/12in or higher.
- Fill the beds with a mixture of soil and well-rotted manure to about 5cm/2in from the top of gravel boards, to avoid soil spillage.
- Pave the paths or leave as grass; or lay a weed-suppressing membrane and cover with a gravel or bark mulch.

especially with perennial weeds, as each broken piece of root left in the soil can grow into a new plant.

Hand weeding may not be a practical option for large tracts of land that are weed ridden. At this stage you need to decide whether to follow an organic or inorganic routine to manage your plot. My advice is: be good to your soil and it will pay dividends. After all, you are what you eat. If you go organic the heritage of your fruit and vegetables will never be in any doubt.

Avoid applying weedkillers unless absolutely necessary, as they pollute the soil (and the vegetables) and may prevent you sowing or growing directly into the ground for some time. If you do resort to chemical controls, choose a product that is as kind to the environment as possible. A glyphosate-based weedkiller, which becomes inert on contact with the soil, is probably the best of available evils. This is applied to the top-growth of weeds and is carried down to the roots, killing the plant permanently from the roots upwards. Use sparingly and follow the instructions. If you decide to use a spray, choose a warm, dry day with no wind, to prevent the spray travelling to nearby plants.

Think twice about trying to clear a large plot in one fell swoop as it is an exhausting task. You can always reclaim a smaller area, covering the rest with old carpet or large sheets of black polythene or membrane (see page 110). The disadvantage of this approach is that the ground will have to lie fallow in this cloaked state for twelve months to make a serious dent on the weed population. However, the job will be easier to tackle, once you are ready, than if the ground had been left open to the elements.

Many advocate rotovating the soil, but I strongly advise against it. If the ground has a large infestation of weeds, chopping up the roots into thousands of little pieces will trigger a whole army of fresh weeds. Rotovate at your peril.

Raised beds in a suburban garden

The soil

Types of soil

The ideal soil for growing vegetables is a rich **loam**, which is fertile, crumbly in texture, high in nutrients, moisture retentive and easily cultivated throughout the year. However, most of us have the soil that accompanied a house purchase or that is indigenous to the allotment, so choice doesn't enter into it! Don't worry: all soils can be radically improved.

Clay is a 'cold' soil, which is slow to heat up in spring. It is wet and sticky (caused by the fine clay particles), poorly draining and susceptible to waterlogging. Clay can be difficult to work in wet weather and freezes in cold months; in dry weather, it tends to crack open. However, clay is naturally rich in nutrients and minerals, making it a productive soil. Incorporating plenty of organic matter or manure greatly improves the structure of clay, making it much easier to work. Cabbages, cauliflowers and broccoli all prefer heavier soils like clay.

Sandy soil is light and gritty. Unlike clay, it is quick to warm up in spring, meaning that crops can be sown earlier, and it is easy to cultivate all through the year. The downside is that sandy soil lacks the ability to retain moisture and nutrients are easily washed out of the soil by rain, so it needs to be constantly replenished with organic matter to keep it fertile and improve moisture retention. Crops that do well in lighter soils like sand include carrots, leeks, onions and parsnips.

Chalk soils are very free-draining, usually have a shallow topsoil, full of flints and stones, and are nutritionally poor. This combination can make it difficult for a plant to get its roots down and establish successfully. Chalk soil also contains lime, which makes it alkaline. Chalk soil needs regular applications of farmyard manure, which is slightly acidic, or other organic matter.

Peat is almost black in colour and found traditionally in fenland and wetland sites. It has a tendency to dry out quickly, so can be prone to erosion, but it is rich in organic material, making it fertile and moisture retentive. Peat soils tend to be acidic.

Acidity and alkalinity

The measurement of a soil's acidity or alkalinity is known as its pH. The scale ranges from 1 to 14 (1 being extremely acid and 14 being extremely alkaline); neutral soil is pH7.0. The majority of vegetables like something in the range pH6.5–7.0 and fruit generally prefers a pH of 6.0–6.5. Soil pH matters more in the vegetable plot than in the herbaceous border because it affects the release of nutrients to hungry crops and can increase the risk of plant diseases such as clubroot (which affects brassicas and is more likely on wet acid soils) or potato scab (which is more prevalent on alkaline soils).

Use a soil-testing kit to determine the pH of your soil. If you are growing on a large area of land, it is useful to take soil samples from different places, to ascertain whether the soil pH is uniform across the plot.

Adjusting the soil pH Correcting pH levels is not complicated. To make an acidic soil more alkaline, simply add lime (see box). Brassicas are likely to be the only vegetables that require lime treatment if the soil is not alkaline enough for them and it will only need doing every three or four years, but carry out periodic tests on the soil, so that you know your pH is within reasonable margins.

To make an alkaline soil more acid, use flowers of sulphur, which can take two to three months to prove effective. Only consider this if your soil conditions are extreme.

Improving the soil

Plants take nitrogen from the soil as they grow and we are constantly removing plant material that would otherwise break down to replace this lost nitrogen, so it is essential to replenish the soil with organic matter regularly to ensure a continuous supply of nutrients to your plants. A good indicator that soil is lacking in humus or organic matter is the absence of earthworms.

Adding well-rotted manure, compost or leafmould improves the available nutrients, structure and aeration of the soil, which in turn aids good root growth and seed germination. It helps prevent soil compaction (the formation of an impenetrable crust on the soil surface that impedes air and water), which is the inevitable result of general cultivation or heavy treading. Improving the soil texture will also reduce the need for constant watering: organic matter acts like a sponge, helping the soil to retain water.

Adding horticultural grit or small-sized gravel is invaluable for soils that are very heavy or compacted, such as clay. The grit opens up the soil, allowing water and air to penetrate more freely. It helps soil to warm up more quickly, increases the rate of bacterial activity and improves water drainage, which is vital to growing healthy crops.

Organic soil improvers

Farmyard manure improves soil structure and adds nutrients. It should be sooty black in colour and have little or no smell; if it has a strong ammonia smell, let it rot down further or it will scorch or damage plants.

Digging over the plot

Apply annually, ideally in autumn on clay soil and late winter or early spring for sandy soils, before plants begin growth. If the soil is very heavy, compacted or waterlogged, dig it into the top 30cm/12in of soil in the first year to speed up the process. Otherwise, dig it in or apply as a mulch (5–8cm/2–3in thick) around plants and let nature do the work.

Leafmould is marvellous for adding bulk to the soil and is rich in micro-organisms and beneficial bacteria. If you have a garden that gathers large amounts of falling autumn leaves, making your own leafmould is an ideal way of recycling them.

Simply collect all these leaves and compost them separately, as they can take a year or more to rot down. Use a covered wire bin or black polythene bags pierced with holes. Water the leaves well and place in a shady spot. Use the rotted leaves as a mulch in autumn or winter or dig into poor soils, about 8cm/3in deep, to enrich the soil nutrients and structure.

Green waste is derived from recycling domestic green waste. It will improve both the structure of the soil and its nutrient levels and, being a recycled product, is an environmentally-friendly option, though not necessarily organic.

Garden compost is simply decayed plant material, so making compost is an efficient way to recycle your garden waste. Any once-living plant material will compost, but avoid substances that attract vermin (food) or don't break down (ashes, tins). Use roughly equal amounts of green and brown plant material to achieve the right balance.

Green material includes grass clippings, vegetable peelings, spent bedding plants, soft green and non-woody prunings, and coffee grounds or teabags. These all rot quickly.

DIGGING

Some of us find digging quite therapeutic, whilst others loathe the task.

Single digging is what most of us do naturally, without even thinking. Grab a nice sharp spade: blunt spades make digging hard work. Work your way along the soil, turning the soil over as deeply as you can practically manage, breaking up any large lumps with your spade. If you have manured the surface of the plot before digging, the manure will naturally be incorporated. My preference is to scatter manure over the entire plot once all the digging is done.

The no-dig method is ideal for the organic gardener and works on the assumption that digging ruins the soil structure. You still have to do preliminary ground preparation to assist aeration, eradicate weeds and eliminate any existing soil compaction but, from then on, soil is never dug. Instead, soil improvers such as well-rotted manure or garden compost are spread over the surface of the prepared ground, leaving earthworms and other soil organisms to incorporate it into the soil.

MAKING COMPOST

There are two composting methods. A hot heap is made all in one go and needs a large quantity of composting material; it heats up and decays rapidly, and will be ready for use within a few months. Cool heaps are built up in layers as material becomes available and will take a year or so to decay.

Hot heaps Make a base layer of woody plants or twigs to aid air circulation and drainage. Fill the bin or build the heap with layers of well-mixed green and brown material, watering as you go. Cover and leave to heat up. After a couple of weeks, turn the heap, mixing well, and add water if it has dried out. Leave for some months until it reaches the desired texture. It should smell earthy, not dank and rotten; sometimes compost can be lumpy and twiggy, but is still ready to spread on the garden even if it hasn't reached the brown crumbly stage.

Cool heaps Start with a base layer, as above, and add enough mixed composting material to make a 40cm/16in layer on top. Cover. Keep adding balanced ingredients until the bin is full or the pile is too big to be comfortably handled. Leave alone. After about a year, check whether the layers are fully rotted. If the top layer is still dry, but the bottom is ready, use the compost that is rotted and re-mix the drier, less decayed material back into the heap, add water, replace lid or cover and wait a few months more.

Do not add perennial weeds such as dandelions, bindweed and buttercups. Nettles are the exception: being very nitrogenous, they act as compost accelerators.

Brown material includes cardboard, crushed eggshells, shredded paper, straw, wood shavings and tough hedge clippings. Woody plant material is slower to decay: if you have a shredder, pass it through that first or chop it up in smaller pieces. Fallen leaves can be composted but are better used to make leafmould as they decay slowly.

Compost bins or heaps (which can handle more material) can be hidden in any corner of the garden. Heaps are best sited directly on the soil or grass, in full sun or partial shade. All compost bins or heaps need lids or a cover of some sort – an old bit of carpet will do in most cases. If you have the space, running several heaps or bins at once will ensure a constant supply of compost and you can use one whilst the other is still rotting down.

Green manures are fast-growing, inedible crops used to fill a patch of land that is bare for six weeks or more, often in winter. They prevent weeds growing in the space and nourish the soil.

Leguminous green manures improve soil fertility by fixing nitrogen into the soil; non-legume manures produce more organic matter and help improve the structure and drainage of the soil. Some manures make lush, rapid growth which is an effective weed suppressant, and some can be left to grow over the winter months, or even for a year or two, cutting repeatedly to encourage new growth and prevent nutrients being leached out of the soil. They are all easy and cost-effective ways of improving the fertility of any soil that is to sustain a vegetable plot.

Efficient recycling using plant waste

GREEN MANURE	SOWING TIME	PERIOD OF USE	COMMENTS
Agricultural lupins (legume)	March to July	10–12 weeks	nitrogen fixing; deep rooting, good for breaking up and aerating soil; cut before flowering
Agricultural mustard (brassica)	March to September	6–8 weeks	no nitrogen fix; weed suppressant; general fertiliser; prone to clubroot; cut before flowering
Alfalfa (legume)	May to July	12 weeks +	nitrogen fixing; weed suppressant; general fertiliser; suitable for overwintering
Annual ryegrass (other)	March to October	12 weeks +	no nitrogen fix; weed suppressant; improves soil structure; suitable for overwintering
Fenugreek (legume)	March to August	8–12 weeks	no nitrogen fix in UK; improves humus and organic bulk content in soil; cut before flowering
Field beans (legume)	September to November	12 weeks +	nitrogen fixing; suitable for overwintering; can be cut once only for re-growth
Fodder radish (brassica)	May to September	6–8 weeks	no nitrogen fix; weed suppressant; general fertiliser; deep rooting, good for breaking up and aerating soil; although a brassica, any crop can follow; cut before flowering
Grazing rye (other)	August to October	6 weeks +	no nitrogen fix; suitable for overwintering
Phacelia tanacetifolia (other)		March to September	10–12 weeks +
Red clover (legume)	April to August	8 weeks–2 years	nitrogen fixing; weed suppressant; attracts pollinating insects; suitable for overwintering; cut after flowering
Tares (Vetch) (legume)	March to September	8–12 weeks +	nitrogen fixing; weed suppressant; suitable for overwintering
Trefoil (biennial legume)	March to August	12 weeks–2 years	nitrogen fixing; suitable for overwintering

Green manures are sown from spring to autumn, depending on the crop. Sow the seed by scattering or planting in drills on freshly prepared, raked ground. When they are ready, simply chop the plants back into the soil a few weeks before planting a vegetable crop, using a spade and slicing up larger clumps as you go. All green manure crops should be incorporated into the soil whilst their growth is still fresh and green and before they start to turn woody (they can take anything from a few weeks to some months to get to this stage).

A word of caution: don't grow a green manure that is a brassica or legume before a crop from the same group, as this can cause disease; so don't plant field beans before pea and bean crops or mustard before brassicas. Other manures can be grown almost anywhere.

Planning the crops

Making plans

First-time growers may feel a bit daunted about what to grow and how many of each plant they will need. Have fun with this: curl up on the sofa, grab a pen and paper and spend some time working out what you'd like to grow and how it will all fit in. The idea is to get the maximum return for the space you have and grow crops for as much of the year as possible.

Space will be the primary decider of what you grow, together with personal taste. Make a wish list of vegetables you like (choose five or so as a start) and work out when they're going to be in the ground, from sowing to harvesting, so you know when you can plant another crop in the same space: sowing and harvesting times are given in the vegetable profiles and on page 126–7. The information about crop rotation (page 102) will also prove useful.

Making the most of the space available

Then add in catch crops such as lettuces, radishes and rocket, and salad leaves or greens as cut-and-come-again crops. Or maybe you fancy a bit of intercropping between the slow-growing vegetables: plant beetroot alongside the parsnips, radishes with cabbages or dwarf beans among sweetcorn. These are all easy ways to get more crops from the same space and vary the produce.

Sowing different varieties of the same crop that mature at different times of the year will keep the plot productive, and successional sowing of the same variety at intervals avoids a glut.

Don't be tempted to buy seed of more crops than you can sow in the available space. I have given an indication of the potential size of each crop in the plant

MAXIMISING YOUR GROWING SPACE

Catch crops are crops that mature quickly (such as radishes, rocket and spinach) and can be slotted in the intervals between harvesting one crop and sowing or planting another. Plant wherever there is spare space.

Cut-and-come-again crops are ideal for the novice or impatient grower. Instead of waiting for leafy greens or lettuces to mature, simply cut the young leaves and they will re-grow, giving several crops of young, tender leaves.

Intercropping is the practice of growing one crop in between the rows, or plants, of another crop. Normally you choose and plant an intercrop that will mature more rapidly than the main crop. For example, parsnips are planted in spring and stand in the ground up to March the following year, but beetroot or radishes can be planted alongside them as an intercrop.

profiles to help you gauge how they will fit into your plot. Cabbages and cauliflowers need a lot of space; if your growing area is limited, look for crops that are small or choose varieties that can be planted closer together.

It is hard to predict yields precisely, because so much is down to the weather, but the profiles give a rough idea of how much the crops will yield, so you can plan the number of plants you will need: work out how many potatoes or cabbages you get through in a week and plant accordingly – bearing in mind that too much of a good thing can put you off! Courgettes, for example, are notorious for giving copious crops and two plants should give you (and your friends) more than you can all cope with.

Choosing varieties Having decided which vegetables to grow, you will be faced with a bewildering array of varieties. If you are working an allotment, ask fellow growers their opinion (they may even let you taste their produce), or ask the commercial seed growers what they recommend. It is a good idea to start with well-known, reliable varieties: as you gain experience, you will develop your own firm favourites and will enjoy experimenting with new or heritage varieties.

Crop rotation

Crop rotation simply means growing different vegetables in different areas of the plot each year. Growing the same crop in the same place every year can lead to an accumulation of harmful pests and bacteria in the soil; crop rotation disrupts the cycle and helps minimise this problem. It is also a reliable way to meet plants' different nutritional requirements: the current crop can benefit from the residual nutrients left by previous crops.

Perennial vegetables, such as asparagus, cardoons and globe artichokes (and the fruits), are not included in a crop rotation plan as they need a permanent site, but other vegetables can be grouped into broad categories which have different cultivation requirements. This helps when planning the rotation of crops. The groups are:

Brassica American cress, Brussels sprouts, cabbages, calabrese, cauliflower, Chinese cabbage, corn salad, kale, kohlrabi, oriental brassicas, oriental mustard, radishes, seakale, sprouting broccoli, swedes and turnips

These require plenty of nitrogen, so are ideal for planting in a patch where legumes (peas and beans) grew the previous year, because the legumes leave residual nitrogen in the soil.

Root vegetable beetroot, carrots, chicory, Jerusalem artichoke, parsnips, potato, salsify and scorzonera, spinach beet and Swiss chard

None of these need particularly high nitrogen levels, so pop them in after a brassica crop.

Legume beans, peas

Nitrogen is one of the most important elements for strong, healthy leaf growth and the roots of peas and beans fix nitrogen in the soil, so it makes sense to plant leafy brassica crops on the site of last year's peas and beans.

Other aubergine, celeriac, celery, chicory, courgettes, cucumber, endive, Florence fennel, garlic, leeks, lettuces, marrow, onions, peppers, shallots, squashes and sweetcorn

All these suffer less from pests and diseases than brassicas and legumes, and will fit nicely anywhere in the crop rotation.

Making a crop rotation plan

Novice growers will find it easiest to opt for a three-year rotation plan, as shown below. The main idea is that you never grow the same crop in the same place over a three-year period.

1 Make a list of the vegetables you would like to grow
2 Sort the list into groups, as above
3 Divide the plot into three segments
4 Follow the planting plan below

Crop plan for year one

Grow root vegetables here
Grow brassicas here
Grow legumes and other vegetables here

Crop plan for year two

Grow legumes and other vegetables here
Grow root vegetables here
Grow brassicas here

Crop plan for year three

Grow brassicas here
Grow legumes and other vegetables here
Grow root vegetables here

Growing

Preparing to sow

Most vegetables are annuals and can be grown from seed. Growing plants from seed is quite one of the easiest things to do. It is wonderful to watch small green seedlings suddenly sprout from the earth and I don't care how many thousands of seeds you may have sown in your lifetime, it is a minor miracle every time when they suddenly emerge, seemingly overnight.

Equipment

You don't really need specialist equipment but there are a few items that make the job a little easier.

- Clean pots and seed trays
- A hand-held seed sower (which makes sowing fine seed easier)
- A soil sieve
- Watering can with rose head for spraying water finely
- Plant labels and a pencil
- A dibber or pencil (or your finger) for planting large seeds and pricking out
- A heated propagator

A small potager-style garden in summer with mixed vegetable-and-flower raised beds

Pots and seed trays As well as standard plastic seed trays, old ice-cream tubs and small plastic pots are suitable for sowing and growing. Root trainers are useful for vegetable plants that resent root disturbance: they avoid the need to disrupt the plantlet's roots by pricking out and potting on. If you have space, cell trays avoid the thinning out process by sowing one seed per cell.

Heated propagators provide gentle bottom heat to emerging plants, encouraging strong root development. A very basic heated propagator that can maintain temperatures of 18–21°C/64–70°F will give reliable results and make a world of difference to your growing success.

Seed

By and large it is better to buy seed every year: old or poorly stored seed can result in variable growing success. Carrots, parsley and parsnips are always best sown from bought seed, and seeds that are labelled F1 hybrids do not come true from saved seed so have to be bought afresh each year. (F1 hybrids are the result of crossing two different varieties, and they are often more vigorous and less prone to diseases than the original plants they were taken from.)

However, you can save seed from your own vegetable crops if they are not F1 hybrids, or trade with fellow allotment holders. Scoop out tomato and squash seeds from ripe fruits but leave pea and bean seeds on the plant until pods are dry and split open. Sweetcorn seed can be variable as it is wind pollinated, so it may not come true. Spread seeds on a sheet of paper in a light, airy place until thoroughly dry, then put in a small paper envelope, label and date, and store in an airtight container in a cool, dry cupboard.

Seed packets contain more seed than you can practically sow and there is always leftover seed; store it in the same way. Most seed remains viable for up to four years if properly stored.

Some vegetables are notoriously difficult to grow from seed, so skip the sowing process altogether: grow Jerusalem artichokes from tubers, asparagus and rhubarb from crowns, seakale from thongs, onions and shallots from sets and potatoes from seed potatoes. All are easily available.

Sowing seed indoors

The British weather is unpredictable, so there are times when we need to extend our growing season. Sowing seed under cover in a greenhouse or polytunnel can give a head start to the crop-growing game. With the luxury of space you can sow many more varieties and, by installing a frost stat, need never worry about cold or frost damage to seeds and plantlets.

Seed of tender vegetables needs to be grown indoors as outdoor temperatures are too cold to allow successful germination: all seed needs water, light, nutrients and ideal temperatures to germinate.

Sowing Sow seed in trays or pots, filled with fresh seed compost gently firmed down. Temperature requirements vary, but 10–20°C/50–68°F is normal for our climate. Check the individual seed packet for details. Seed that benefit from heat to germinate are ideal subjects for a heated propagator.

Try not to handle seed too much. Sow straight from the packet, using it as a funnel, or shake a small amount into your palm and scatter it evenly, randomly and lightly on the surface of the compost. Cover with a thin layer of compost at a depth of no more than twice the diameter of the seed (a small soil sieve is useful for this, as it gives even results). Water and label clearly.

DAMPING OFF

Seedlings grown indoors are susceptible to a fungal disease known as damping off. This normally occurs in poorly drained, wet or cold conditions and can cause seedlings to shrivel and die. Water a drench of Cheshunt Compound lightly over the soil before sowing, and keep sowing conditions hygienic: ensure pots are clean, the greenhouse is well ventilated and there is adequate warmth. Sow seed thinly to avoid overcrowding and don't overwater.

Watering Use clean water for watering indoor seedlings: rainwater from butts may contain bacteria that can exacerbate damping off. Water with a fine rose attached to the watering can, or you will disturb the emerging seedlings, and always water from above. Water regularly, keeping compost moist but not soggy and allowing pots or trays to drain freely. Never use icy water as this can chill the seedlings.

Thinning It is possible to sow one seed per pot, if the seed is large, but few of us have enough space to grow seeds in this way. Sowing in compost trays or pots gives rise to a rash of young seedlings: thin seedlings when the tray is overcrowded by pulling out the poorly growing ones, leaving the stronger, sturdier looking seedlings space to develop without competition, so they can grow on, ready for pricking out and transplanting.

Pricking out This refers to the removal of strong young seedlings from a tray to an individual pot where they will have more growing space. Don't wait until the seedlings are too overcrowded to do this as they will grow weak and spindly.

When each seedling has two true leaves, lift it individually by the leaves, never the stem, and use a dibber to lever the roots up gently. Transfer the seedling to a pot of fresh compost, keeping handling to the minimum. Firm the soil gently around the roots with a dibber or pencil to prevent air pockets, water well and label.

Hardening off Plantlets are hardened off about two weeks before transplanting outdoors to acclimatise them to lower outdoor temperatures. Move them from the greenhouse to a cold frame, cloche or polytunnel, which will act as a halfway house before they are planted into their final outdoor positions. Expose them to outdoor temperatures for a couple of hours a day by opening vents or windows, and gradually increase their exposure over a two-week period.

Transplanting Plantlets are ready to transplant when they are a reasonable size (they will look exactly like miniature plants). Some are moved straight into their final growing positions outdoors, but most are hardened off first.

Dig a hole about the same size as the pot; loosen the plant gently, trying not to disturb the rootball, and set into the ground at about the same level as it was growing in the pot. Press the soil gently but firmly around the base of the plant, water in well and label the newly transplanted row.

Sowing seed outdoors

One for the blackbird, one for the crow,
One for the cutworm and one to grow.
Anon

Pre-warming the soil in spring before direct sowing extends the growing season and accelerates seed germination, particularly if you have cold, heavy soil. This technique is especially useful when growing tender crops, such as peppers, sweetcorn and tomatoes.

Place plastic sheeting (pegged down), portable cold frames or cloches over the growing areas, both day and night, for a couple of weeks before sowing to increase the soil temperature.

Dark-coloured, organic matter (well-rotted manure or garden compost, for example) added to the soil absorbs sunlight during the day, naturally raising the temperature (as well as improving soil structure and nutrition levels). Raised beds tend to retain heat better than open ground.

Sowing in seedbeds A seedbed is a small area of the vegetable plot set aside as a nursery for seedlings. It should be sited in an open, sunny position and protected by barriers or chicken wire to prevent cats using it as a litter tray! It needs well-drained soil that is raked to a fine tilth and kept well watered and completely weed free. Scatter (broadcast) or sow seed in labelled rows and wait for it to germinate. Thin seed where necessary and grow the best seedlings on until they are large enough to transplant into final growing positions.

Sowing in drills This is the traditional sowing method for vegetables that have small seed and are sown outdoors in their final growing positions. It is also used for the many vegetables that are deep rooting (carrots and runner beans) or resent root disturbance (calabrese and kale) as direct sowing avoids the need for transplanting.

A drill is a shallow furrow, made by scraping your hoe or spade edge along the soil surface in a straight line (mark it out with a string line first). Water the bottom of this shallow channel thoroughly to aid germination, allowing it to drain fully. Sow seed thinly along the length of the drill and cover with sieved, dry soil. Firm back the soil after the seed is sown, water thoroughly again and label the row clearly. The emerging seedlings will be in a uniform straight line and can't be mistaken for weedlings.

Station sowing Large seeds, including those of cucumbers, squashes and melons, are best station sown. Two or three seeds are planted together in one hole, at the final spacing, and later thinned to one seed. This avoids the need for excessive thinning, as you are only planting three seeds at intervals along the row. Of course, you can plant single seeds, but planting two or three at once gives an insurance policy if the others should fail. This is also a good method when using more expensive seed as there is less waste.

Clump sowing Some vegetable seed (beetroot, carrots, leeks and turnips, for example) can be bought as multigerm seed (four or so seeds in a cluster). Multigerm seed can be thinned, but the advantage of seed clusters is that they reduce the time spent sowing and thinning. Left alone, they will produce a group of baby-sized vegetables.

HAND POLLINATION

Pollination is the exchange of pollen between plants so they produce seed. Certain vegetables, such as marrows or aubergines, may need pollinating by hand when they are growing and flowering under cover, where the pollinating insect population can't gain access to them; outside, nature will do it for you.

It's easy to do: use a fine paintbrush and transfer the pollen from the male stamen and stroke it lightly over the female stigma. For marrows, take a male flower (this has a thin stalk behind the petals) and remove all its petals, then press it against the centre of the female flower (this has a tiny marrow behind the petals).

Thinning This is the removal of surplus seedlings in the row, allowing the remainder plenty of space to grow and develop. Thin seedlings when they are large enough to handle, keeping the strongest seedlings for transplanting to final positions later. Don't worry that you are throwing the surplus seedlings on the compost heap: you can only properly care for a limited number of plants. Seed tapes (lengths of pre-spaced seed) are now more commonly available and do away with the need for thinning.

Spacing Crops need space in order to develop properly, maintain healthy air circulation and allow access for weeding, watering and thinning. The amount of space between plants in a row and between rows of plants is calculated on the eventual height and spread of the proposed crop; sowing spacings are given in the profiles to help you plan your crops. Many growers use a bamboo cane or notched plank to reduce the time required for marking out. When the plants are mature, the leaves should be just touching.

Double rows are an excellent way of growing more in a restricted space. The leafy cover of the plants (typically peas and beans) shades the soil, which stops water loss and helps keep weeds down, and the plants may provide some support for one another. Double rows may simply be two rows sown more closely together than usual; for deep-rooted plants, make a shallow trench or furrow 20cm/8in wide and plant seed along both edges of the furrow; cover gently and water in.

BOLTING

Bolting means that a plant flowers early and rapidly goes to seed before a crop matures, which can render a whole crop inedible. Bolting can be caused by various weather conditions: dry weather causes cauliflowers and spinach to bolt; other crops, such as oriental mustard, can be affected by cold weather; and annual crops (chicory, endive and lettuce, for example) can bolt if sown too early. Grow bolt-resistant varieties where possible and sow seed at optimum times to reduce the risk.

Be gentle when hoeing between rows

EARTHING UP

This simply means drawing earth up around the base of a plant as it grows. Potato plants need earthing up to prevent light turning the tubers green, as green potatoes are poisonous. Plants such as Brussels sprouts, cabbages or Florence fennel also benefit from earthing up to give them extra support, and celery, Florence fennel and leeks are earthed up to blanch (whiten) the stems.

Watering

Growing crops need a reliable source of water to keep them thriving, healthy and productive. Watering has become a hot issue of late, particularly in areas affected by hosepipe bans and because of the changes in our climate. Water conservation needs to be a major consideration, because it is utterly heart-breaking to watch young, burgeoning crops shrivel and die from lack of water.

Feeding

Just like us all, plants need to be fed. Fertilisers feed the plant rather than improve the structure of the soil, supplying extra amounts of the main nutrients that plants require.

Nitrogen (N)	Encourages vegetative growth, important for leafy crops
Phosphorus (P) (phosphates)	Essential for root development and fruit ripening
Potassium (K)	Essential for healthy fruit formation

Minor nutrients such as iron, manganese zinc, boron, copper and molybdenum are also needed, but in minute quantities: deficiencies of these are uncommon.

If growing areas have been prepared with organic matter, the need for additional nutrients should be minimal. There are no two ways about it: incorporating organic matter and compost into vegetable growing beds may seem like hard work initially, but it will save a lot of effort later on, and your crops will be all the more prosperous for it.

However, fertiliser can be very beneficial on a plot that has been neglected, and nitrogen levels may need topping up during the growing season for some crops. Leafy vegetables like cabbage require high levels of nitrogen, as it is being constantly used up by the plants. If plants are spindly and slow growing and the leaves start yellowing, they are suffering from nitrogen deficiency and will benefit from a quick fix of fertiliser, but it is important to remember that fertilisers are not a substitute for improving the texture, structure or water-holding capabilities of the soil by adding organic matter (such as well-rotted manure or garden compost).

Organic fertilisers are derived from plants and animals. They include chicken manure, bonemeal, hoof and horn, fish, blood and bone, and seaweed extracts. Inorganic fertilisers are derived from chemical manufacture. Whichever route you choose, they all contain the three basic soil nutrients (nitrogen, phosphorus and potassium) and some will also contain manganese, boron and other trace elements. Follow the application instructions for all fertilisers and you won't overdo the dosage.

CONSERVING WATER

To make water go further:
- mulch, to retain moisture in the soil
- water in the early morning or evening, so water is not wasted by evaporation in the sun
- water at the base of plants, to direct water to the roots where it is needed
- water liberally once or twice a week, rather than giving mean amounts more frequently
- use shade netting over young crops, to prevent evaporation and reduce the amount of water they need
- invest in water butts: they make all the difference in times of water shortage
- use seeping hose, to soak the ground gently and efficiently around the roots of plants
- avoid digging in dry weather to prevent soil drying out from wind or sun exposure

Fruit and vegetables thrive side by side

Boron deficiency can affect all sorts of crops; including beetroots, brassicas, carrots, cauliflowers, celery, radishes, swedes, turnips and fruits. The symptoms differ depending on the crop: stunted, yellowing leaves and hollow areas of stem in cabbages; root splitting in carrots; brown or poorly formed heads in cauliflowers; distorted leaves or splits in the outer stalks of celery; brown or grey ringing in the harvested roots of swedes and turnips; poor, stunted growth and undersized fruits in strawberries. To remedy, apply a borax solution to the ground before sowing or planting.

Manganese deficiency is indicated by yellowing between leaf veins that then develop brown patches, or circular brown spotting on the leaves of peas and beans. Brassicas, beetroots, parsnips and tomatoes, and many soft and tree fruits are also vulnerable. It is more common on acid or poor-draining peat soils, so don't overlime vulnerable soils. Spray plants with manganese sulphate.

QUICK-FIX TONICS

Foliar feeding is an efficient way of delivering a dose of nutrients when a deficiency becomes evident. The tonic supplements any soil feeding and is sprayed on to the leaves, both top and undersides, and allowed to drip off.

Granular or slow-release fertilisers are scattered on the soil and are comparatively fast acting. They are particularly useful for a shot of nitrogen (for vegetative or leafy growth) or potassium (to encourage flower or fruit formation).

Potash deficiency in potash-loving fruit and tomato crops is seen as brown scorching on the leaves, and fruit that is mean or blotchy. A soluble application is available to correct the deficiency.

Organic fertilisers

Blood, fish and bone is a traditional, finely ground fertiliser, containing bonemeal, dried blood and fishmeal, enriched with potash and other plant foods. It provides a balanced feed, encouraging healthy root and top-growth.

Bonemeal is a popular, traditional fertiliser that is high in phosphates and also provides nitrogen; it stimulates root growth and development, so is especially good for peas, onions, potatoes and root crops.

Chicken manure is good for leafy plants as it is high in nitrogen. It is bought as pellets which are spread around the base of plants and watered in or forked into a moist soil. Nutrients are released into the soil as water and moisture breaks the pellets down, and are taken up by the roots.

Comfrey leaves are very high in nitrogen and make an excellent mulch or liquid feed for vegetables. To make your own, fill a plastic tub with leaves, add water to the top, cover with a tight-fitting lid and leave for five weeks. The stewed leaves are marvellous accelerators on the compost heap; drain off the dark, wicked-smelling, murky liquid, dilute 10:1 with water and use as needed. Comfrey pellets are available from organic suppliers.

Hoof and horn is a concentrated, long-lasting, nitrogen-only fertiliser, especially good for leafy vegetables. It can be used from spring to autumn.

Weeding

Weeds rob the soil of moisture, light and nutrients that are otherwise destined for your vegetables. They can be annual (including suspects such as groundsel, chickweed and fat hen) or perennial (ground elder, couch grass, bindweed and nettles).

Annual weeds are easy to get rid of. The trick is never to let them flower, as the flowers produce seeds that will create a fresh generation of weeds. Hoe the seedlings mercilessly or pull them up if they grow beyond this stage.

MULCHING OPTIONS

Mulches can be successful in preventing weeds (see page 97), though the level of attractiveness is hugely variable!

Polythene sheeting (or old plastic compost bags) prevents weeds emerging; it also holds moisture in the soil and can be useful for raising soil temperatures before sowing seed. Peg down, and make slits in the plastic to plant through.

Cardboard and newspapers can be laid in layers over beds, between the crop rows. Wet it first (too much water and it will turn into papier mâché!) and anchor with soil, bricks or grass cuttings. It lasts so well that you may have to tear it to shreds and add it to the compost heap once it has served its purpose.

Grass clippings, spread 5cm/2in deep, keep weeds down: don't apply thickly or you will be left with a dense, sodden mass.

Pruning waste, shredded in a garden waste shredder, is effective for covering paths and walkways but is not useful for mulching crops because of the high wood content (which takes nitrogen from the soil).

Ornamental mulches such as cocoa shells, pebbles and gravel can all be used on paths. Ornamental bark is best employed as a path cover rather than a vegetable bed mulch, as it robs nitrogen from the soil.

Perennial weeds are a tougher proposition; their root systems will re-grow even when the top-growth is removed or dies back in winter. Perennial weeds usually need digging up, rather than pulling out, and it is very important to get up the entire root system as even fragments of broken root can give rise to new plants. Weed perennials relentlessly and meticulously.

Hand weeding with a small fork works well in smaller areas; a Dutch hoe, also known as a cutting or push hoe, is the most effective for weeding in larger areas, and hoeing bare soil will prevent weeds emerging. Heat torches can be used to zap the top-growth of weeds, so they wilt and die, but this is impractical in large areas.

Growing in containers

All sorts of vegetables can be grown in containers and you'd be surprised how productive they can be. Beetroot, dwarf beans and peas, carrots, garlic, potatoes, tomatoes and strawberries can give worthwhile crops in small spaces.

Growbags are large plastic sacks filled with a growing medium suitable for vegetables and are used for growing vegetables that don't have deep roots, such as aubergines, chillies, cucumbers and tomatoes. I have a friend who grows lettuces in them very successfully. The average growbag will accommodate two or three plants. They can be used outdoors, in small spaces such as balconies and sheltered roof terraces, or in greenhouses.

When growing in pots, you will need crocks to cover the drainage holes, a good-quality compost, and possibly bamboo canes to stake taller plants. Whichever medium you choose, growbags and pots will need to be kept weed free and well watered.

Companion plants such as chives can be planted in pots and moved easily to a susceptible crop

Fruit trees

Fruit trees are widely available from commercial growers: invest in certified disease-free, vigorous healthy plants to ensure you get off to a good start. Most fruit trees are grown on rootstocks – that is, they are grafted on to the roots of another plant; the graft union is at the knobbly joint in the trunk.

Grafting enables growers to control the eventual size and crop of a tree, and may also improve disease resistance. All you have to do is ask the nursery for suggestions and choose a tree whose size suits your plot.

Pollinators

Many fruit trees are self-fertile (that is, they can produce a crop of fruit with their own pollen). However, others are not. Put simply, an apple tree usually needs to be fertilised by another apple tree to produce apples, and the two trees need to flower at roughly the same time for fertilisation to take place. Crab apples, such as 'Golden Hornet' or 'John Downie', are reliable pollinators for most varieties of apple tree. If in doubt, ask your nurseryman for advice.

Pruning

Left to their own devices, fruit trees will produce quantities of leafy growth at the expense of fruit, so one reason for pruning is to encourage fruiting. Pruning also governs the size and shape of trees; it makes them infinitely manageable and encourages health and vigour. Pruning a tree or bush hard (removing more growth) results in the plant making strong new growth; light pruning involves taking away less growth and the plant responds by producing moderate new growth: prune strong growth lightly and weak growth harder.

> **TERMINOLOGY**
>
> All trees have a trunk. The main branch that rises skyward from the middle of the trunk is called the central leader. Branches grow out from the trunk, lateral stems grow from the branches and smaller side shoots grow from the lateral stems. At the end of every branch there is a long, thin, tapered shoot, known as the branch leader. A spur or fruiting spur is a short stem, coming off a branch, that bears the fruit buds.

Pruning times

The pruning process applies to all fruit trees, but timings vary according to the crop.

Apple and pear trees are pruned in winter (November or February), to establish the framework and encourage new growth. Once established, free-standing trees are only pruned in winter; cordons, espaliers and fans are pruned in summer (July or August).

Stone fruit trees such as apricots, cherries, peaches and plums are pruned once a year: young trees in March, as the buds burst, and established trees in June or July. The timing is critical, to reduce the risk of disease such as silver leaf.

Formative pruning

The first reason for this type of pruning is to determine the eventual shape and size of the tree. Pruning fruit trees is important in the first five years as this is when the permanent framework is formed. Formative pruning is done when trees are dormant, ideally immediately after planting (or in March for stone fruits, as explained above). Container-bought plants may be planted outside the dormant season; wait until the appropriate season before formative pruning.

Fruit trees can be grown into various forms. In open spaces, trees are a good choice; in restricted spaces, espaliers and cordons are perfect for apples and pears, or fan shapes for cherries, peaches and plums.

Young trees will produce fruit, but only allow three or so to ripen for the first three years. Pick the rest off in July to allow the tree to develop fully.

Pruning for fruit

There are two kinds of buds on a fruit tree: growth buds (which produce non-fruiting growth, i.e. stems) and fruit or flower buds (which are where the fruit is 'set' or develops). Fruit buds are normally larger than the slimmer growth buds. Left to itself, a tree can produce too many fruit buds, leading to numerous meagre fruits or a crop so heavy that the tree struggles to cope and its limbs may break.

Making a pruning cut

Always use clean, sharp secateurs or loppers so that all pruning cuts are neat, to allow for quick healing. To prune stems and side shoots, make a sloping cut just above an outward-facing bud, or a straight cut above a pair of buds.

To remove a larger branch, start by making a shallow cut in the underneath of the branch, about 10cm/4in away from the main trunk, and then saw downwards from the top of the branch until both cuts meet, to sever the branch cleanly from the tree. Try not to leave any torn stubs (smooth them down with a garden knife). Paint cuts of more than 1cm/½in with wound sealant.

Spur pruning Most fruit trees are spur bearers. After the first two or three years, fruit buds form spurs along the branches. These can get crowded, so the fruits don't have enough room to develop (there could be ten or more fruit buds on the spurs after five or six years). Cut off the lower fruit

---

FORMATIVE PRUNING FOR TREES

When growing a tree in a natural, unrestricted way, as you might see in an orchard, the aim is to produce a goblet or vase-shaped tree that is open in the centre above a clear stem (imagine placing a large inflatable beach ball in the central hollow on top of the trunk, with the branches cradling the ball, and you will have a good idea of the shape you need to achieve).

After planting This first stage is ideally carried out immediately after planting, if planting coincides with the tree's pruning season (see page 113 for pruning times). The young untrained tree will be a very slender trunk with small branches coming off it. With a sharp pair of secateurs, cut off the top part of the main stem, making a sloping cut just above a bud. Cut at the following heights, depending on the form you intend to grow:

Bush tree	75–90cm/2½–3ft
Half-standard tree	1.2m/4ft
Standard tree	1.5m/5ft

This decapitation process may seem drastic, but do it anyway! It is an essential part of creating the framework. You should be left with a central stem with five or six main branches coming off it, spaced around the tree like spokes of a wheel. Remove any shoots that are visible below this main framework, using a sharp pair of secateurs and cutting close to the trunk. This will leave a clean trunk.

At the end of year one Cut back the main branches by half or one third: this will produce secondary branches next year. Always prune to an outward-facing bud.

At the end of years two and three The primary or older growth and secondary, new branch framework of the tree will now be clear. There is no need to prune the older growth unless it is damaged or diseased. Cut the new side shoots by a third, pruning to an outward-facing bud.

By the end of this process, the primary and secondary framework has been established.

TRAINING FOR OTHER SHAPES

Fruit trees and some soft fruits can be grown in a variety of ways to enhance their ornamental appeal, but training can also improve cropping: for example, peaches and apricots need the protection of a warm wall to grow well in this country. For training against a wall or on wires, buy a partly trained three-year-old tree with eight or more branches.

Cordon A single-stemmed tree or trees, normally grown at a 45° angle; fruit is produced on short spurs along the trunk's length. Cordons are ideal where space is restricted or as an ornamental feature and are no more than 2–2.5m/6–8ft in height.

Espalier Similar to a cordon, but the tree is grown in an upright position and longer horizontal branches are trained from each side, resembling tiers, and tied to horizontal wires, so it is normally trained against a wall. It can have a number of side tiers, from one to as many as five or six. One-tiered espaliers can be used very successfully as low step-over apples, providing a charming border for a potager or as path edging. They have a height of 2–2.5m/6–8ft and spread of 3m/10ft.

Fans Apples, cherries, gages, nectarines, peaches, pears and plums can all be grown as fans, though this method is more commonly used for apricots, peaches and nectarines that require the warmth of a sheltered wall. Fan out the branches in equal spacing from the bottom of the trunk and tie in to horizontal wires, fixed to the wall, as they grow. They have a height of 2–2.5m/6–8ft and spread of 3m/10ft.

Cordon   Espalier   Fan

spurs as close to the stem as possible, reducing the spurs to four or five buds, pointing upward. This will allow four or five good-sized fruits to develop, instead of lots of little mean ones. Repeat every few years, as necessary.

Tip pruning Some apple and pear tree varieties, especially those that have a weeping habit, bear fruit at the tips of young shoots: these are known as tip bearers. They tend to be light croppers and only need maintenance pruning. Don't snip off the tips or you'll get no fruit!

Maintenance pruning

Once a free-standing tree is established, prune annually to maintain the open shape by cutting out any crossing branches and removing the three ds: dead, damaged and diseased wood.

Trees may need renewal pruning; remove old branches that aren't fruiting well to allow new ones to grow in their place. Also remove branches that are hanging down to the ground or are too high to manage: cut the branch as close to the trunk as possible, using a saw to make a sharp, clean cut. Always use wound paint on large pruning cuts to prevent infection.

Wall-trained fruit will need replacement pruning from time to time. Cut out any old, poorly fruiting growth and replace them by tying in newer, more vigorous young shoots to fill the gap.

Problems

All plants are going to be affected by pests and diseases at some time. After all, if your produce is attractive to you, it's not surprising that insects and wildlife think it looks pretty good too! But believe me, so many troubles can be avoided by good plant husbandry and vigilance.

Look after your soil. Healthy growth depends on a healthy soil: the better the structure of the soil, the easier it is for plants to thrive (and the better they will come through dry periods). Feed the soil rather than the plant: this leads to stronger growth and improves resistance to pests and diseases.

Practise good plant and plot hygiene. Clear away plant debris, remove diseased material as soon as you spot it and keep weeds down so they don't overcrowd plants.

BENEFICIAL WILDLIFE

Encourage the natural enemies of garden pests into your plot. Many insects and animals will help keep down garden pests and maintain a healthy garden environment.

- Put up nesting boxes to encourage birds, who are voracious bug eaters. Unfortunately birds also have a penchant for stealing fruit, so ensure crops are netted, and supply bird feeders as decoys.
- Make a shallow pond or fill half a water barrel to attract frogs and newts, which hoover up garden pests. Leave a small log pile in a redundant corner to encourage hedgehogs and productive insects such as lacewings to overwinter on your plot, where they will prey on garden pests.
- Sow some wildflowers to attract bees, which are vital for pollinating crops.
- Plant dill to attract hoverflies a-plenty: they do a terrific job of eating aphids.
- Mulch the soil to increase beneficial bacteria and micro-organisms.

FROST DAMAGE

Frosts can catch the blossoms and flower buds of fruit trees and bushes, turning them brown and pulpy and preventing proper fruit development. The foliage of leafy vegetable crops can also be vulnerable to frosts: frosted leaves blacken and wilt.

Avoid planting any fruit or vegetable crops in frost pockets or east-facing sites that are exposed to early morning sun. Protect vulnerable fruit trees, such as peaches, by training them against warm, sunny, sheltered walls and try growing varieties that flower later and so are less vulnerable to a touch of frost.

Using organic garden practices means that produce will have a clean bill of health. Most pests can be dealt with by hand-picking the culprits from the crop or parasitic nematodes are available for slugs and snails (and are child, pet and bird friendly). Chemical sprays are not the smartest thing to use on food crops and should be avoided.

Above all, be vigilant: examine leaves for signs of damage or for munching bugs and take effective measures immediately. Don't wait, or a small problem can escalate into something pretty unmanageable.

Fruit and vegetable pests

Physical barriers

Birds (particularly pigeons), mice and squirrels all like to feed on crops. Protect fruit crops with bird netting and vegetables with horticultural fleece; prevent mice nibbling seed and crops by setting traps; spray squirrels with a hose if they are really pesky, and hang wasp traps in trees.

Natural pheromone traps and grease bands are available to help check pests on fruit crops and special cabbage root fly mats can be laid around the base of the plants, to prevent cabbage fly laying their eggs.

FRUIT AND VEGETABLE PESTS

Aphids are a group of pests about 2mm/⅛in long and ranging in colour through black, grey, green, white and yellow, including blackfly and greenfly, black bean aphid, cabbage mealy aphid, cabbage whitefly, currant blister aphid, onion thrip and many more. They feed on the sap of young shoots of fruit and vegetables, causing the leaves and stems to curl and distort. The growing tips are mainly affected.

Rub off small infestations with your fingers or spray with warm soapy water. Chemical sprays are available.

Big bud mite looks exactly as it sounds, with overlarge buds containing numerous white mites. Leaves and stems often don't develop well and this pest particularly affects blackcurrants.

Remove all swollen buds by hand and destroy them. Dig up and burn seriously affected plants.

Brown scale The brown scales of these sap-sucking mites can be found on stems of fruits such as apricots, figs, grapes and peaches, particularly when grown against sunny walls or in greenhouses. Secondary infections such as sooty mould may set in.

Spray trees and bushes with tar oil in winter.

Cabbage root fly larvae feed on the roots of brassicas; transplanted plants are the most vulnerable. Leaves develop a blue tinge and wilt for no apparent reason; young plants can die.

Place plastic or cardboard collars round the base of young plants.

Capsid bug is a sap-sucking green bug that feeds on the shoot tips of crops such as apples, currants, gooseberries, pears and plums.

Check plants regularly and spray with recommended insecticide.

Carrot fly is a small, shiny black fly that attacks carrots and parsnips. The adult female lays eggs around the plant base in early summer and early autumn and the creamy-coloured larvae (1cm/½in long) tunnel into roots, causing them to rot. Leaves develop a red tinge and stunted growth or wilt occurs.

Sow seed in June to prevent an early summer attack or sow under cover. The smell of bruised foliage attracts the flies, so sow thinly to avoid thinning (and bruising) later. Growing carrots between onion rows and companion planting with African marigolds will put the carrot fly off the scent.

Caterpillars The most common culprits on vegetables are the caterpillars of the cabbage white butterfly and all moth caterpillars (known as cutworms), but all caterpillars are dealt with in the same way. They feed on vegetable and fruit tree leaves, often leaving unsightly holes, and the roots and stems of beans, cabbages, carrots, celery, leeks, lettuces, peas and potatoes. Silky webbing on leaves is an indicator they are present, although they are usually easily visible to the naked eye.

Pick off by hand; for a large infestation on a few leaves, remove the leaves and destroy them. Chemical controls are available.

Celery leaf miner feeds on the foliage of parsnips and celery, leaving leaves scorched and brown. Celery may become bitter tasting.

Remove all affected foliage and destroy. There are no chemical controls for the home grower.

Codling moth lays her eggs on developing fruit around June and the larvae tunnel into the fruits (apples, pears, quince and, rarely, walnut). Biting an apple may reveal the maggot or grey tunnel left by the emerging caterpillars. These have white bodies and contrasting brown heads and tend to overwinter in the bark of fruit trees.

Remove caterpillars by hand and dispose of them. Nematodes are available that are sprayed directly on to the caterpillars, and there is a solution that is sprayed on to the tree bark to prevent overwintering. Otherwise spray young or small trees with a recommended insecticide.

Cutworm see **Caterpillars**

Flea beetle is a small, shiny black beetle (about 3mm/⅛in long) that attacks the upper surface of a leaf, causing small, round, shallow holes; the affected areas may shrivel and brown. It mainly affects young seedlings of Brussels sprouts, cabbage, cauliflower, kale, radish, rocket, swede and turnip. A heavy infestation may kill seedlings or stunt growth of more mature plants.

Keep plants well watered and tended to encourage rapid growth of the seedlings, as more mature plants are less susceptible. Chemical controls are available.

Gooseberry sawfly larvae are the slim, bright green, sometimes black-spotted sawfly larvae (very like caterpillars) that eat the leaves of gooseberries and red- and whitecurrants. If the infestation is severe, the whole plant can lose its leaves almost overnight.

Check plants meticulously from mid-spring onwards, especially at the centre of the bush, where you may see signs of eggs along the veins of leaves. Remove all affected leaves, with larvae or eggs, and destroy them.

Leatherjackets are the browny-grey grubs of the crane fly (daddy long legs). They live in the soil, eating any seedlings and the stems and plant roots of strawberries, lettuces and brassicas, especially from August until the following May, and ultimately causing plants to wilt and die.

Encourage natural predators such as birds into the garden or use a biological nematode that can be watered into the soil, killing the grubs.

Onion fly It's not the flies you need to worry about, but their maggots, which eat onion roots and bulbs and may cause plants to suddenly yellow and keel over, especially in summer.

Cover crops with fleece to prevent the fly laying its eggs. Onions grown from sets are less likely to succumb.

Pea and bean weevil is a tiny greyish insect that munches on leaves, leaving semi-circular notching that is unsightly but rarely fatal.

Spray with insecticide if infestation is heavy.

Pear and cherry slugworm These slug-like larvae of the sawfly munch the foliage of cherries, pears and quince, turning leaves skeletal and brown.

Pick them off or spray with insecticide from spring to autumn.

Plum sawfly lay their eggs on plum flowers in spring and are a serious pest. The young maggots tunnel into the fruits and feed on them from the inside, causing a sticky, black ooze which weeps from holes in the skin. Fruits fall from the tree long before they have time to mature.

Dig the soil at the base of the trunk to expose overwintering pupae to feeding birds.

Potato cyst eelworm is a very common pest that affects potatoes and tomatoes and is especially prevalent when crops are not rotated. They are invisible to the naked eye and develop in the roots of crops. Symptoms include stunted or poor growth, leaves may yellow, and small white pustules or cysts can be clearly seen on the roots.

The microscopic eelworms can survive in cysts in the soil for many years, so practise crop rotation to prevent them building up in the soil and grow resistant varieties. There are no chemical controls available for the home grower. Lift potatoes as soon as they are ready to limit the spread of cysts on the roots. Remove and burn affected plants, including weeds from the same area. Don't transplant affected plants and don't add affected material to the compost heap.

Raspberry beetle affects all cane fruits, such as tayberries, loganberries, blackberries and, of course, raspberries. The brown adult beetles (about 3mm/⅛in long) lay their eggs on the flowers in early to mid-summer and the young grubs make their way into the developing fruits. Berries turn grey, normally at the stalk end first, and the fruit wizens and dries.

Sticky traps that catch the adult beetles are available for organic growers.

Red spider mite is a sap-feeding mite which affects both indoor and outdoor plants and is hardly visible to the naked eye. Leaves suddenly yellow and silky webs appear around the leaves and stems of plants.

Spray the underside of leaves with an upturned hose from the start of the growing period. Biological controls such as *Phytoseilus persimilis* are successful if introduced early in the season. Red spider mite is very resistant to chemical sprays.

Slugs and snails have a legendary appetite for leafy material. Look for slime trails and leaf damage: leaves that are munched close to the bottom of the plant are more likely to have been attacked by slugs; top leaf damage is more commonly inflicted by snails, who don't mind the climb!

Place small plastic trays filled with beer or other sweet liquid around crops; the slugs and snails are lured by the sugary liquid and drown in it. Parasitic nematodes (supplied as a powder that is mixed with water to activate them) burrow under the skin of slugs and kill them; or sprinkle organic slug pellets sparingly around plants; these kill slugs or snails on contact and are harmless to birds, pets and children.

Winter moth caterpillar damages the blossoms of fruit trees and bores its way through fruits.

Apply grease bands around tree bases in autumn to prevent the female moth climbing the tree and laying her eggs. Pick off caterpillars or spray with an insecticide when buds open.

Wireworm is a six-legged worm, about 2.5cm/1in long and golden brown. It lives in the soil, eating through the roots and stems of seedlings and young plants such as lettuces and root vegetables, including carrots, potatoes or turnips, causing plants to wilt and die.

They attack maturing vegetable roots, so harvest crops as early as possible and destroy any worms. There are no chemical controls available to the home gardener.

Woolly aphid is a brown, sap-sucking aphid with a waxy coating, found in late spring and summer in small woolly lumps, normally around old pruning cuts in apple trees. Its activity can make trees vulnerable to canker infections.

Spray with a recommended insecticide (though their wax coating makes them resistant to sprays); washing up liquid mixed with water helps break down the waxy armour.

Fruit and vegetable diseases

No matter how good your garden hygiene, you are bound to encounter the odd disease. Plant diseases are not as easy to spot as the common garden pests: it can be difficult to recognise that a plant is sickly, let alone find the cause of the trouble. Following some simple guidelines can often prevent nasty conditions spiralling out of control.

TIPS FOR DISEASE-FREE PLANTS

- Grow disease-resistant varieties wherever possible.
- Keep plants well watered and mulched to prevent roots drying out: caring for plants with regular watering and feeding equips them with stronger disease resistance.
- Avoid planting too closely together, to improve the airflow around plants.
- Hygiene in the greenhouse and garden is an obvious deterrent to plant sickness. Clear up fallen leaves, where fungal diseases can overwinter and make sure seed trays and pots are washed before use and that garden tools are clean.

FRUIT AND VEGETABLE DISEASES

American gooseberry mildew is a white, powdery fungal growth that can appear on stems, leaves and fruits, particularly of gooseberries and blackcurrants. Although unsightly, crops remain edible.

Prune out affected growth and thin branches to improve air circulation. Avoid nitrogenous feeds, using a general fertiliser instead. Grow disease-resistant varieties when possible.

Apple powdery mildew is more common on apples, but also affects pears and quince. Leaves are covered with a white powdery fungus and young leaves are particularly vulnerable. Growth may be stunted or distorted.

Prune out all affected growth and keep the branch framework open and airy to encourage good air circulation. Annual mulching and regular watering will help prevent the onset of the disease. Fungicidal sprays are available.

Bitter pit in apples is caused by calcium deficiency: the skins develop sunken (pitted) brown spots and the apples taste slightly bitter.

Use balanced general fertilisers rather than high-nitrogen feeds. Mulch the base of trees to preserve moisture in the soil. Spray developing fruits with a recommended calcium solution.

Blackleg is a bacterial infection that mainly affects potatoes, but can also affect stored root vegetables, such as carrots. Infected foliage turns yellow, stems turn grey/black and collapse, and the tubers turn slimy and rot.

Grow disease-resistant varieties where possible. Dig up and destroy any infected plants and the original seeding tubers. Practise crop rotation.

Blossom end rot is an effect of calcium deficiency, normally caused by poor watering. The skin at the bottom of tomatoes blackens or browns, causing the roots to dry out.

Pick off any affected leaves, stems or tomatoes and destroy them. Water plants well and regularly.

Blossom wilt is a fungal infection that affects apples, apricots, cherries, peaches, pears and plums. The flowers and leaves brown and wither, appearing scorched, but they remain on the tree, causing spurs and branches to die back if left untreated. Fruits may be small and shrivelled.

There is little to be done once a tree is infected. Limit damage in subsequent years by pruning out affected twigs and removing diseased or damaged fruit and any affected plant debris that has fallen from the tree. Do not store any affected fruit and do not pull any stalks from fruit you are intending to put into storage.

Botrytis (grey mould) is a very common fungal infection that strikes unhealthy plants and flourishes in damp or poorly ventilated conditions. It can survive on live plants and on dead or decaying plant tissue, and affects many types of plant. Grey, fluffy mould containing spores is clearly evident and will disperse in the air, spreading the spores, if handled carelessly. It can also enter plants through wounds, causing leaves to brown and soften before becoming covered in the grey mould.

It is difficult to control as it is spread through the air, but good growing conditions and plant hygiene do much to prevent it. Remove affected parts, cutting back to healthy growth, and burn or dispose of infected material – but do not add it to the compost heap. Fungicidal sprays are available.

Cane spot is a fungal infection, prevalent in June, which affects blackberries, raspberries and hybrid bush fruits. Inky brown spots with silvery middles appear on canes, spreading to leaves and flower stems. Left unchecked, canes will split and die.

Grow disease-resistant varieties. Prune out and dispose of infected canes. Spray with fungicide.

Cankers Bacterial or fungal cankers affect fruit trees and look similar, causing shallow depressions to form on the bark, normally near a pruning wound or near buds. Growth can die back and fruit may rot.

Remove affected fruits, prune out dead spurs and shoots in summer and burn all diseased material. Grow disease-resistant varieties. Spray with Bordeaux mixture or a copper-based fungicide in August, and again in September and October.

Clubroot can reduce a grown man to tears. It is a soil-borne infection affecting all vegetables in the cabbage family and is almost impossible to control as spores remain in the ground for years and are carried on boots and garden tools. Symptoms include wilting leaves and yellowing, stunted growth. An affected plant has swollen, club-like roots.

As preventive measures, ensure the ground is well drained, maintain an alkaline soil and practise crop rotation. Remove and burn all affected plants. When growing plants from seed, use fresh, sterilised compost and well-scrubbed pots. A clubroot drench or dip is available.

Cucumber mosaic virus is a common virus affecting cucumbers, aubergine and a wide variety of other plants. Leaves are mottled green and yellow, the leaf surface tends to crinkle and plant growth is distorted and stunted. Fruits may not develop or may be small, hard and pitted with bright yellow splotches.

Destroy affected plants and do not handle healthy plants after touching them. Grow disease-resistant varieties. There are no chemical controls available to the home grower.

Dieback is a fungal infection affecting tree and bush fruits, caused by drought, poor watering or waterlogged conditions. Symptoms are wilting, yellowing foliage. Parts of the plants die back, but it rarely affects the whole plant.

Prune out and destroy all affected shoots or stems and improve hygiene by regular watering and soil drainage.

Downy mildew is a fungal infection caused by humid, damp conditions that affects brassicas, lettuces, onions, and many root vegetables. Symptoms are browning or yellowing of the upperside of leaves, with fluffy mildew or mould on the undersides. Though not usually fatal, it is unsightly and weakens the plant. If not caught early, *Botrytis* (grey mould) can set in.

Remove and destroy all affected leaves, water plants from the base and avoid overwatering; try to improve air circulation by sowing thinly in the first place.

Fireblight is a bacterial infection that affects apples, medlars, pears and quince. Early symptoms are flowers wilting and dying quickly. If left unchecked it can travel to infect stems, leaves and branches. Normally it sits randomly through the tree, not just in one place.

Cut back all infected plant material to healthy stems and wood and burn all prunings. Wash tools after use to prevent spread. It is fairly uncommon but there are no chemical controls available to the home grower.

Fruit splitting (the skins and stems split) is caused by erratic watering, too much watering or sudden temperature changes.

Water regularly; mulch plants to maintain moisture in the soil.

***Fusarium* wilt** is a fungal condition largely affecting pea crops, where stems can suddenly and unaccountably wilt. Telltale signs are sudden yellowing of leaves that then turn brown, normally from the bottom of the plant upwards.

Remove and destroy all infected leaves or plants. Rotate crops to avoid build-up of fungus in the soil; grow disease-resistant varieties where possible.

Halo blight is a bacterial infection affecting bean crops, with leaves developing a yellow halo or rimming. If left unchecked, leaves die and bean pods develop grey patches and the crop will be reduced.

Destroy all affected plants immediately. Water plants at the base, avoiding splashing the leaves, which can spread the infection. Don't grow the seed from affected plants, and grow disease-resistant varieties when possible.

Onion neck rot is a fungal infection that causes onion necks to rot. It can occur after onions are harvested.

Dry harvested onions thoroughly. Onions grown from sets are less likely to be affected; practise crop rotation as a preventive measure.

Onion white rot is a soil-borne fungal infection that can stay in the soil for years, affecting chives, onions and leeks. The bulbs rot and are covered in a white mould, and the plant collapses and dies.

Pull up the infected plants, burn or dispose of by sealing in plastic bags (including the soil surrounding each plant, as this contains resting fungal matter). Do not put on the compost heap, and don't plant any of the allium family in the same soil. Practise crop rotation as a preventive measure and grow disease-resistant varieties. There are no chemical controls available to domestic growers.

Potato blight is a fungal infection that occurs in moist, warm, humid conditions and can be serious if left untreated, wiping out an entire crop. Leaves develop brown patches, with white fluffy fungus on the undersides, and then shrivel and die. The potatoes may develop dark patches, leading to rotting flesh.

Plant disease-resistant varieties. Remove affected leaves immediately and earth up the stems, to prevent spores falling on lower leaves. Spray with a copper-based fungicide, such as Bordeaux mixture or mancozeb as a preventive measure.

Potato common scab Beetroot, potatoes, radish, swede and turnip are all vulnerable to this fungal and bacterial infection. Tubers develop rough, slightly raised scabbing on the skin, but damage is usually superficial: you just have to peel your potatoes more thoroughly. It is more prevalent on light, sandy soils, or over-limed soils.

Don't lime soil before planting; add organic matter instead. Water regularly in dry or drought conditions and grow disease-resistant varieties where possible. There are no chemical measures available.

Rhizoctonia (plant rot) is a soil-borne fungal disease affecting celery and Florence fennel, causing stunted growth and lesions on the bulbous parts of the plant, which leads them to rot.

Dig up all affected plants and dispose of them. Don't plant any of these crops in the same spot for at least three years. Spraying seedlings with a copper fungicide can make crops less vulnerable.

Rots The stems and leaves as well as the roots and fruits of many crops are prone to fungal and bacterial rots, usually caused by too much watering or watering from above.

Remove the damaged areas or the whole plant and destroy. Maintain good drainage and ventilation. Water regularly.

Rusts become evident in damp weather conditions and can affect a wide range of fruit and vegetables, including leeks. Brown, yellow or orange spores are visible on the leaves or stems.

Water regularly and increase or improve air circulation by not overcrowding plants. Remove all diseased foliage and burn. Apply a copper-based fungicide to protect currant and gooseberry crops, but generally there are no controls available to the home grower.

Scab is a fungal infection that affects fruit trees, particularly apples and pears. Leaves are small or fall off, and the fruit is small and distorted, with brown scabby patches, and may split.

Cut out affected areas, remove and destroy all debris. Grow disease-resistant varieties and prune to keep the centre of the tree open. Spray with fungicide.

Sclerotinia rot is a fungal disease with fluffy white growth affecting Florence fennel and lettuces, fruit stems and tubers, arising in damp conditions. Leaves at the base of the plants turn brown and soggy and plants may wilt and die.

Dispose of and burn all affected plant material. Don't grow plants prone to *Sclerotinia* in a spot that has been infected for at least four years.

Silver leaf is a fungal infection that affects stone fruit trees: leaves develop a silvery lustre and the inside tissue of stems or branches may reveal brown stains. Pruning cuts are the most common cause, allowing the spores into wounded branches; it is spread by rainfall, splashing, and dirty pruning tools.

Cut infected wood back to the point where there is healthy white tissue and prune in summer when trees are less vulnerable to attack. Grow disease-resistant varieties when possible.

Tomato blight is a fungal infection similar to potato blight, caused by moist, humid conditions. Symptoms are the same, with curling, blackened leaves.

Destroy infected material. Treat with a copper-based fungicide such as Bordeaux mixture or mancozeb as a preventive measure. Plant disease-resistant varieties where possible.

Verticillium wilt is caused by several types of *Verticillium* fungus and affects aubergines, strawberries and fruit trees. The foliage wilts in isolated places and the crop is reduced.

The only thing to do is dig up affected plants with their soil and burn them. Don't plant susceptible plants in the same place for several years. There are no chemical controls available to the domestic gardener.

Violet root rot affects leafy vegetables, such as celery and asparagus, but beetroot, carrots, potatoes and parsnips are also vulnerable. Roots and tubers are crowded with purple filaments, bearing fruiting bodies that fall into the soil, spreading the disease. Leaves are stunted, deformed and yellowing.

Dig up and burn all infected plants (this could mean an entire crop). Practise crop rotation as a preventive measure.

White blister is a fungal infection that affects all the brassicas, salsify and scorzonera. Leaves yellow and develop powdery white blistering on the underside.

Remove and destroy all affected plant material. Avoid overcrowding plants, to allow good air circulation, and water plants at the base to avoid soil splashing the leaves.

The gardening year

Spring

Traditionally spring is a very busy time for the produce gardener: it is the official start of the growing season. The weather may be unreliable early in the season, but you can begin sowing seed in the greenhouse as well as pre-warming your soil with cloches in readiness for outdoor sowing and transplanting a little later. March and April are an ideal time to start an asparagus bed and your early potatoes can go in. The spring cabbage will be nearly ready for cutting as you bid a fond farewell to the last of the previous year's sprouts, winter cauliflowers and swedes.

Whatever the tasks, spring is a gloriously optimistic month for the home grower with all the anticipation of the delicious produce you will be bringing to your table. And at this time of year you are not under attack from the pests or diseases that are more prevalent in later months and can blight both confidence and crops. Clean out the potting shed or greenhouse, roll up your sleeves, sharpen your hoe and put a good edge on your spade – the growing season is under way!

A flourishing potager garden

Summer

Weeds can be rampant at this time of year, so stay on top of them as you busily check and thin your crops and keep a watchful eye on the watering front. Plant outdoor tomatoes in a sunny spot and sow your maincrop peas, carrots and French beans now there are no frosts to threaten them.

The vegetable plot is full of bounty in summer and as you harvest salad leaves, lettuces, spring onions, radishes, early carrots and early ripening strawberries you will feel your exertions have all been worthwhile. Yes, sometimes it is tiring; your back often aches, those weeds did seem particularly vexing and perhaps the blackfly got to your broad beans. But the whole growing process allows unique moments of achievement, pleasure and relaxation that cannot be derived anywhere else. Summer is a-coming in, as they say, so pat yourself on the back, enjoy the delicious fruits of your labours and start limbering up for the next wave of seed sowing.

Autumn

The year winds slowly down from September and a more relaxed pace prevails. You have already enjoyed the tasty novelty of your earlier crops and the sweetcorn should be ready any day, but many of your crops will be coming to an end. Like all good veggie gardeners, you will probably be wondering how to fill your winter table. You have yet to harvest cauliflowers and dig up maincrop potatoes, and now is the time to sow spring onions and winter lettuces, as well as plant out spring cabbage for next year.

You will have hit your stride by now, feeling a bit of a dab hand at all this sowing, transplanting and gathering caper and no doubt will be mentally sizing up some crops you have never grown before for next year.

As bare spaces emerge, you can fill the gaps with quick-growing salad crops

Winter

If you are well organised, you may still be contentedly planting garlic or new fruit trees and gathering buttery coloured parsnips sweetened by frosts, sleek, straight leeks and fresh, crisp Brussels sprouts. With your produce stored nicely for winter and your plot emptying, this is an excellent time to dig over the ground, incorporating lime or manuring soil, before the weather becomes perishingly cold.

The year has been productive and you have worked hard, so give yourself a well-deserved rest, retire to the sofa with a cup of tea and some good seed catalogues, and let your mind drift to the year ahead. As you thumb through the colourful catalogues with their enticing descriptions, you can be confident that those wonderful seeds will be growing into the finest feast for miles around next year.

Monthly planner

KEY　　●●●● sow indoors　　●●●● sow outdoors　　●●●● plant　　●●●● harvest

Vegetable	Jan	Feb	Mar	Apr	May	Jun	Jul	Aug	Sep	Oct	Nov	Dec
Artichoke, globe												
Artichoke, Jerusalem												
Asparagus												
Aubergine												
Bean, broad												
Bean, French												
Bean, runner												
Beetroot												
Broccoli												
Broccoli, sprouting												
Brussels sprouts												
Cabbage, autumn												
Cabbage, Chinese												
Cabbage, red												
Cabbage, spring												
Cabbage, summer												
Cabbage, winter												
Cardoon												
Carrot												
Cauliflower, autumn												
Cauliflower, spring												
Cauliflower, summer												
Cauliflower, winter												
Celeriac												
Celery, leafy												
Celery, self-blanching												
Celery, trench												
Chard, Swiss												
Chicory, Belgian												
Chicory, radicchio												
Chicory, sugarloaf												
Corn salad												
Courgette												
Cress, American												

KEY ●●●● sow indoors   ●●●● sow outdoors   ●●●● plant   ●●●● harvest

Vegetable	Jan	Feb	Mar	Apr	May	Jun	Jul	Aug	Sep	Oct	Nov	Dec
Cucumber												
Endive												
Fennel, Florence												
Garlic												
Kale, curly												
Kohlrabi												
Leek												
Lettuce												
Marrow												
Mibuna												
Mizuna												
Mustard, oriental												
Onion												
Onion, spring												
Parsnip												
Pea												
Pepper, chilli												
Pepper, sweet												
Potato												
Pumpkin												
Radish, summer												
Radish, winter												
Rocket												
Salsify												
Scorzonera												
Seakale												
Shallot												
Spinach												
Spinach beet												
Squash, summer												
Squash, winter												
Swede												
Sweetcorn												
Tomato												
Turnip												

Plant index